Without the Smell of Fire

Other Writings by Walter Lanyon

A Lamp unto My Feet ◆ A Light Set upon a Hill
A Royal Diadem *and* Leaves of the Tree
And It Was Told of a Certain Potter *and*
Abd Allah, Teacher, Healer *and* Embers
Behold the Man! ◆ I Came
Impressions of a Nomad ◆ It Is Wonderful
London Notes and Lectures
Out of the Clouds
Quintology: Ask and Ye Shall Receive
That Ye Might Have ◆ The Eyes of the Blind
The Impatient Dawn ◆ The Joy Bringer
The Laughter of God
The Temple Not Made with Hands
Thrust in the Sickle
Treatment *and* Demonstration *and* Your Heritage

Without the Smell of Fire

Walter C. Lanyon

Without the Smell of Fire

Mystics of the World First Edition 2017
Published by Mystics of the World
ISBN-13: 9781946362186
ISBN-10: 1946362182

Cover graphics by Margra Muirhead
Printed by CreateSpace

Walter C. Lanyon, 1887–1967
Originally published 1941

Contents

DEDICATION ... 7
THE VIRGINAL MIND ... 9
I AM IMMORTAL ... 19
VENGEANCE IS MINE ... 23
THE SECOND COMING ... 30
PUTTING ON THE VESTMENTS OF YOUR OFFICE ... 38
"NEITHER DO I CONDEMN THEE" ... 44
THE PATTERN ... 48
THE HOST ... 52
THE ECHO ... 57
BUT HOW DID IT EVER HAPPEN? ... 64
THE POWER OF THE "LET THERE BE" ... 70
THE PRISON HOUSE ... 76
NONE OF THESE THINGS MOVE ME ... 81
RETURNING TO THE ALMIGHTY ... 84
YET IN MY FLESH ... 88
TO HIM THAT HATH ... 91
FOLLOW ME ... 95
ASCENSION ... 98
WITH ALL THY GETTING ... 104
CONSCIOUSNESS ... 111
THE ANSWERED PRAYER ... 116
NOTES ... 125
FEAR ... 128
THE WAY OUT ... 134
REVELATION ... 142
HOW IT IS DONE ... 148
BEWARE OF PICKPOCKETS ... 154
THE INSPIRED PRESENCE ... 163
ABOUT THE AUTHOR ... 175

DEDICATION

This book was born in Miami, amid flaming hibiscus, on golden sands beside turquoise waters, beneath sunny skies and green palm trees casting their purple shadows. It was born of Spirit, as free as a lovely gull soaring into the limpid depths of the morning. No sooner was the annunciation made of its coming than a body was provided for its advent. So this book is dedicated to all this loveliness and to the Giver of the body.

I have called this book *Without the Smell of Fire* because I have been so impressed that the time has come for the vast army of truth students to advance to that state of expression where the "smell of fire" of the trials and problems through which they have gone be gotten rid of.

Without the scars of battle or the smell of fire about them should they advance into the New Day of recognition, wherein the former things are passed away. It is time we laid aside the cocoon of human thought from which we came. We are the cosmic beings, awakening to the glorious fact that we have always been just that. The smell of fire of the trials through which we have come is absorbed in the glorious light of Spirit. Our garments are made clean, and even the memory of our trials is fading away. We stand on the mountaintop of revelation. We are born again into the old secret that we were created in the image and likeness of God and have been sojourning in the hell of human thought for many years.

Arise, then, and put on the "vestments of your office," forgetting those things which are behind and pressing on into a fuller and more glorious expression of your cosmic Being. Your name is Wonderful now because you have discovered your real Self.

THE VIRGINAL MIND

Mary, the virgin, was overshadowed by the Father. The annunciation was made, the conception took place, and the impossible happened.

Every manifestation of God takes place through this same medium, the virginal mind being overshadowed by the Father. The moment this is clear to you, you will understand why your efforts have met with such small returns. You have tried to overshadow the adulterous human mind with the Father-Consciousness, and no conception could take place. The mind which Jesus said was "a liar and the father of it" cannot receive the pure Spirit; hence, nothing takes place but the malformations of human thought.

No matter what intensity of light you pass through a green glass, the effect will eternally be the same: everything will take on the nature and color of the glass. No matter what light you try to pass through the adulterous mind of John Smith, the results will always be in the limitations of John Smith, and nothing can be done about it until it is clearly understood that "I can of mine own self do nothing," that the human mind is capable of doing nothing but evil and that taking thought is entirely outside the regulations or revelations of Jesus Christ. "Who (do you know anybody?) by taking thought can add one cubit," and "if you cannot do that which is least…? You must answer this question before you can proceed to the virginal mind of Mary.

Jesus realized he could do nothing with the human mind of Jesus. He knew that if he were to bring forth any manifestation of God, he would have to enter into his heritage of Spirit, and in that pure pristine consciousness of eternal virginity, he could receive that overshadowing of the Father and the immaculate conception would take place. No amount of thinking will accomplish this, for it is impossible for a person blind to think of receiving sight. He has never had sight; he is not capable of thinking anything about it intelligently. Yet the man born blind did receive his sight, and he did it at the instant of being able to believe. This belief, in his case, was something outside of human thinking. It was a sudden recognition of his spiritual identity, his heritage of immortality, the virginal consciousness which Mary represents.

It is wonderful when you glimpse for a moment this particular function which instantly takes place the moment you recognize that thinking will not and cannot enter into the place of the impossible. With all this, there is such a simplicity that the child can take it and you cannot, because you, in your magnificent intelligence or the poverty of your thought, cannot believe the impossible. You have not the capacity in a finite thought-taking consciousness to conceive the infinite. The child can take, just as Jesus did, but the adulterous mind cannot because it is so filled with the limitations of human thought. Generations of evil thinking have so filled the thought-taking mind with fear, belief, disease that it cannot function in the next dimension, where "I am of too pure eyes to behold iniquity" is the law.

There is nothing strange, mystical, or unusual about this wonderful union of virgin and Father-Consciousness. It is just a recognition that it can happen. "Whatsoever I can tell the Father in secret I can call from the housetops." In other words, whatsoever I can *accept* will be given a body and form. The child is born.

How is the child to be born? Entirely outside the laws of man. It is a birth which is to entirely set aside every preconceived notion of how it is done. It is a consciousness

The Virginal Mind

which transcends all the workings of the human thought. In fact, it is the impossible—yet is it the possible. It is established on the Earth with such unexpected swiftness that no human thought can stand in its presence. It is, in fact, the way of bringing heaven to Earth, a discovery of that which has always been a sudden entering into a natural heritage.

The moment you perceive the difference between the third-dimensional human mind and the consciousness which operates from the "it is consummated" standpoint, you will find you are in the virginal mind of purity into which the seed is immediately sown, and by magnifying the Power and not questioning further, you will know the conception has taken place. Nothing can happen to the adulterous mind of human thought. "You must decrease; I must increase." The old human thing that left the Garden of Eden to find a kingdom of thought finally gives up and returns to pure consciousness—virginal consciousness overshadowed constantly by the Father, who is pouring out unlimited manifestation.

It is all too good to be true—that is why it is true. And it is so simple it is difficult. The moment human thought touches it, it is not, for nothing you think can in any way approach this thing which is above thought. You understand that everything Jesus did was done from the standpoint of consciousness, which he said was simple enough for a child to possess. No healings were ever made that did not take place through a sudden elevation to the virginal mind. Even the beggar at the temple gate, with his forty years of evil thought, suddenly answered the call, "Rise and walk." This was quite impossible to him.

It was either *rise and walk* or remain with the thought condition. And so is it with you. You either hear and obey, *outside of thought*, or you think about it. But gradually the human mind gives up, and you begin to "enter in" and are saved.

"I will go unto my Father." Why don't you go in and possess this Consciousness which you left so many years ago for the hell of human thinking? Answer me. Do you *believe* or do you "believe"?

Nothing is going to happen, for everything has already happened, just as in the case of Jesus when he said, "Thank you, Father, I knew this was already done." The movement of the "it is done" consciousness into the flesh is automatic and enters into fulfillment by the way you *know not of.* The virginal mind of Christ was immediately overshadowed by the Father-Consciousness and brought forth. So conscious was Jesus of this that he immediately brought forth the immaculate conception—that manifestation which was impossible to the human thinking plane.

Suddenly man arises from the filth of human thinking; he goes in and shuts his door and begins the simple prayer of Jesus: "Be still, and know that I am God." A contemplation of God more and more establishes the Presence, until you have one God here, there, and everywhere and eternally available. It is easy enough to find God in things good and beautiful, but you are to discover Him in hell, in your problem, your enemy, your disease, and the moment you do, the embodiment begins to appear.

It is all beyond human thought. "I come at a moment you think not." The power is not invoked by human thought. It is an *entering in* and acceptance of the fact that *God is*, in contradistinction to the idea that God *has to be* established by argument and affirmation.

Whenever the true affirmation is made, it is a statement that proceeds from the "it is done" consciousness, and the confirmation immediately takes place. The moment you are anything in consciousness, at that moment the confirmation takes place on the outside, and they call you

The Virginal Mind

by your new name. So that instead of trying to make yourself something you are not, by affirmation, words, lessons, etc., you suddenly enter into what you actually *are*—an appropriation. The annunciation having been made, the desire forms in the mind which is the thing in its incipiency waiting to be born. All it needs is the virginal consciousness that can believe. This will accomplish the work, and the desire will be embodied.

Formerly we thought that a desire was given us and had to be worked upon. Today we know it is merely the announcing angel which says, "Mary, Mary, Mary—unto you a child is to be born." It says to you that the desire that is in your mind at the moment is to take place the instant you can enter into the virginal consciousness of "I believe"—I accept; I appropriate without question, without wanting to see whether it works or not.

If you "try" this or think to "prove it," nothing happens but a distorted idea. Or the desire enters into the *symbolical* world, and you have another unborn child—a child without a body, a desire without fulfillment. Thousands of people in metaphysics have a world full of symbolical things, dream things. They are rich in mind—powerful, well, etc.—but there is no embodiment, and that is because the virginal mind was never ready to take the overshadowing of the Father-Consciousness. It is all so wonderful and true that the kingdom of heaven on Earth is made up of the consciousness which can *believe* and appropriate above the human thinking basis of life.

You have already brought out all the "possible" in your human life. You are trying to do the impossible, yet you insist on doctoring up this old human mind and trying to patch up the old garment. New wine in old bottles destroys the bottles and wine. Stop working with problems; stop trying to "get things," and enter into your Consciousness and be free. This appropriation is not difficult. It is just an "outside" of human thinking dimensions. If you do not *believe* in God, then all your work is purely mental and will get you nowhere.

Many people believe God is simply for the purpose of solving their problems, at the same time finding that a combination of men, politics, business, or disease can keep them from entering into the kingdom of heaven.

If you know of any man or situation that can keep you out of your heaven, then you know of something that is stronger than God, and you should fall down and worship that greater power. If there is anything that can hold out against God and win, then that is the thing for you to worship.

Do you believe in God? *Or do you?* And if you do, enter into your Consciousness and be free. Arise and "go unto your Father" and let your problems and cares pass away for the moment. When you return, you will find every measure you have held to the universe full, pressed down, and running over. It is too good to be true, but it is the way of Jesus Christ, and it is possible—yes, possible to you. Do you believe in God? Or is your little intellect or your great intellect stronger? Does it know of a disease that is stronger than God, and does it know of a situation stronger than God? And can it prove in a thousand ways that "it cannot happen?" Then you must bow down to that power, become its "yes man," and you will be rewarded after a fashion.

"Arise and shine, for thy light is come, and the glory of the Lord is risen upon you." This is something that must be done in consciousness and not in thinking, because you have tried for forty years at the gate of your temple to do just this very thing and have failed. So if you are to arise, you will have to arise beyond the level of human thought. Just as an invalid in a burning hospital suddenly finds full use of her limbs which for years have been impotent, just

The Virginal Mind

as the beggar at the temple suddenly jumped out of a thought formation of forty years the moment his thought was taken off of the situation, so you will suddenly see—and when you see, *you will see*. It is something beyond thought, reason; it is the "foolishness in the eyes of man," for everything that God stands for and represents to man is foolishness.

Man supposes that God is there as a reason to build churches and have organizations, which will fight among themselves and fall down to a personality. "Awake thou that sleepest, and Christ shall give thee light." This Christ is your virginal consciousness, which gives light to the temple so filled with the creations of human thinking, so cluttered up with the history of your case. It is wonderful what this Christ-Consciousness in you can and does do, the moment you *let* It and the moment you cease to "try" or "prove it."

As long as you are trying to prove God, you do not believe, and your doubt throws a curtain of opaque thought in the way of manifestation. All the manifestations in the Bible were done at the point of sudden *entering into* the virginal consciousness. The age of your problem has nothing to do with the question. It is only as old as the last thought you have about it. There is no more age to your disease than the last thought about it, no matter what pictures it has piled up on the screen of your body. The instant the thought is broken, at that instant the pictures disappear.

Always to remember the ease with which this is accomplished is to take away all anxiety from the picture. It is easy, it is natural, it is normal on the plane of your Christ-Consciousness, but it is difficult and impossible on the human thought plane. It is wonderful when this light begins to break over you; you enter in, and the chattering of the human mind has ceased.

The human mind has tried to build its tower to heaven and ended in a barrage of meaningless words. This pathetic story is your story, trying to build a tower to heaven which was on the Earth and all about you. How blinded and hypnotized we have all been by human thinking. "There is nothing good or bad but thinking makes it so." But the things of consciousness do not come under this category. They are not of the fluctuating nature of thought—they are of changeless substance. Yet "as a man *feels in his heart*, so is he" explains perfectly what the acceptation of consciousness will cause to happen. There is no question of maybe or perhaps or anything of the kind. As he "thinks in his *heart*," so is he. Do you begin to grasp the consciousness of it all? And are you able to enter in with so small a thing as a grain of mustard? Do you begin to perceive?

Do you begin to glimpse this virginal mind, the Mary consciousness, which is ready for the seed of something that is impossible? If so, you are at the frontier of your *new* country and are ready to enter into a place of great revelation. "Believest thou that I am able to do this?" And the Mary consciousness answers, "Yea, Lord," and the glorious conception takes place. "Behold, I come quickly and my reward is with me." The whole manifestation in its entirety takes place. It does not come under the law of "work out your own living by the sweat of your brow." It is born of God and it is so.

Can you understand why there will be hours and moments and days when your prayer will be a constant recognition of God Almighty and you will utter silently, "My Lord, and my God." You will finally come into the kingdom of heaven, and the former things will pass away.

So transformed will your life become by entering into your spiritual heritage and appropriating the kingdom of heaven within that "they will know you no more." So great

The Virginal Mind

will be the transformation that the thoughts and things of yesterday will be wiped out.

The moment you have dropped anything from your consciousness, it is dropped from manifestation, and all those who bear witness against you are gone. You have no accusers because you have stopped accusing yourself. It is wonderful, this glorious entering into the virginal mind which is ready and willing to accept anything that the Father—your Father-Consciousness—wishes to bring into manifestation.

Jesus standing before five thousand hungry men, as unable to do anything about the situation as you would be: "I can of mine own self do nothing." Jesus entering into the virginal mind of Christ, the dimension of the impossible: "I go unto my Father." Nothing is impossible to this Consciousness. Jesus returning to the personal with the consciousness "it is done" and seeing the empty measures of belief filled, pressed down, running over until there were twelve hampers of bread left over. Where did the hampers come from? Where did the bread come from? Did it all happen, anyway?

The old adulterous mind wants to know how it is done, so it runs about to see a man instead of a principle, and it always comes back with a surfeit of that man. "What went ye out for to see?" Answer me. You will never see a miracle, because you cannot accept it. In the adulterous human mind, it is not possible to *see* anything outside the dimension of thought. You will never see the increase or the supernatural taking place. The only thing you will see is that the unexplained phenomenon is a "coincident." You may be able to explain it all away by thought. "If you deny me, I will also deny you." If you deny your Christ, the return of this denial will be apparent in your limited manifestation of good.

Without the Smell of Fire

The virginal mind is that elevation which can believe without question, without measuring anything by thought, just as the child takes its good without question of the possibility or source. You have that mind in you which was also in Christ Jesus. It only needs recognition, and the moment you can "believe" from this virginal consciousness, the conception takes place.

The Word which enters into the flesh "comes quickly," and it brings its body with it. You take your embodiment with you into the new expression. Soul and body are at last united in flesh, and this fleshly temple is the place to *see* God. It is through this temple-body that the unseen is stepped down into the seen. The child is born. The "I believe" consciousness has been appropriated, and you hear the annunciation of Spirit: "Mary, Mary, Mary—unto you a child is to be born."

Unto you a new desire is to take shape and form, and it is to be outside the law of man. It is to come through by the law of God. It is to be released by a way ye know not of. It is so.

I AM IMMORTAL

Voltaire once cynically remarked, "Since God created man in His own image, how often has man endeavored to render a similar service to God?"

> I am immortal. I am not of this world. I am birthless, ageless, deathless—without beginning or ending. I am born of Spirit—I am Spirit. I make myself as God, even as did Jesus, thereby assuming his true identity.

I am immortal. Created in the image and likeness of God, with dominion over all things, all things are placed under my immortal Self. I am immortal, created a little lower than the angels (the power which flows direct from the Godhead into expression). All things are placed under my feet (understanding, realization). I have but to make the assumption of my immortal Self to find myself possessed of full authority over the transient patterns of matter.

At the moment of recognition of my immortal Self, I am in authority: "I say unto one, Go, and he goeth, and to another, Come, and he cometh." The recognition of my immortality vests me with the power to disintegrate any and all patterns of evil, no matter from what cause. At the coming of this light, the shadows of evil are automatically dispersed. This is the effortless, unlabored action of light.

No resistance is possible, no struggle necessary. I have but to conceive of my immortal Self to see this take place. The congestion of human thinking which results in evil has no more intensity than the thought back of it. It is sustained and fed by thought, having no other reality. The recognition of my divinity does not set up a counter force to evil. There is no battle between good and evil which takes place in the Spirit. At the recognition of immortality, the patterns of human thought automatically disseminate.

Without the Smell of Fire

I am immortal. I call no man my father but one, who is in heaven; therefore, I instantly drop out of expression all thought and patterns of environment, heredity, race consciousness—they all go by the board.

I am of too pure eyes to behold the iniquity of human thinking as a reality. I am free from the hypnotism of history, race, creed, or established beliefs, however time-honored. I am immortal—I am not of this world, yet am I in it.

My body is the temple of the living God. I am filled with the ageless life and light of God. This light in the midst of my temple searches the joints and marrow. It is a living well of water in the midst of me, cleansing, purifying, and washing away all pictures of disease, age, evil. I am birthless, ageless, deathless—without beginning, without end. I am immortal.

I am immortal. I live in the changeless realm of Spirit. I see through all thought-pictures of separation. I AM THAT I AM has sent me into expression, unhindered. I am God in essence. I am one with God. I make myself as God.

I am immortal. I live in the abode of pure Spirit. No plague can come nigh my dwelling. No pestilence of human thinking, no dishonesty or cunning of the human mind can stand. I go forward and backward; I unfreeze the evil patterns of the past, which I accepted as real. I regain all losses from whatever cause; I repossess all apparent losses; I retake my own.

There is no law of the past, no matter how well established, that can withstand this Light. The dishonesty, craftiness, of any and all human minds toward me is consumed; it is utterly confounded, dumbfounded, put to shame. It makes no difference how this inconveniences the human mind which perpetrated the evil. The law of Light will force the corrected manifestation to take place. Nothing can withstand this immortality. All things are revealed in this Light. Nothing is lost, stolen, or taken from the One. I therefore "go in and possess the land" (the consciousness of my immortality).

I am immortal. The evil of human belief which came at me in one way will flee in ten, glad indeed if it will have any way of escape.

I am immortal. I go before, preparing the way. I absorb all patterns of future fears. I destroy all barriers and obstacles that human fate may have placed before me. I go to prepare a place. Nothing can withstand the brightness of my coming.

I am the Voice. I speak, and it is done. At the tone of my voice, all other voices cease. The babbling, chattering voice of matter is still. The malicious, venomous tongue of the serpent is silent. When he would speak evil, he suddenly finds himself utterly voiceless. Every evil that he has spoken returns to him with accelerated force. He is now in the midst of a hell of his own creating, peopled with his venomous desires fulfilled. He shall remain in dumbness and confusion until he perceives the light. His voice shall no more be heard in the land.

I am immortal. Everything that is true is eternal, real—here and now. I perceive this at the moment of recognition, the moment I call upon my Father. There is no time—no waiting, no begging or beseeching—only recognition. The moment I enter into the consciousness of immortality, I live, breathe, move, and have my being in God. I perceive all things as they are. I perceive the finished and completed idea, even as the slow human thought is dragging through its interminable pictures of evil. I know now, from this elevation, that the answer is before the question; the flower is before the seed. The more I magnify this power the more I see the processes of materialization stepped up. "The fields are white," even while the slow human thought is knowing that it takes four months to bring about the harvest.

I am immortal. "The wisdom of man is foolishness in the eyes of God." Nothing it says, does, or believes has any authority except that given it by human thought. It therefore makes no difference how the human thought is inconvenienced, turned awry, twisted, confused, or thrown back upon itself.

I am immortal. I see the restoration of all things taking place. The years that the locusts of human thought have eaten are restored. I live in a world of Spirit; I am no more under the curse of the law. The only thing I have to do with is Spirit, in one form or another. The moment I become conscious of this, the congested patterns of human thought lose all power. All things therefore respond, cooperate, assist, and in every way help the revealing of the kingdom of heaven on Earth.

I am immortal. I am clothed in my right mind, sitting at the feet of God.

VENGEANCE IS MINE

When I was a child, my mother said to me one day, "Son, God has relieved you of one great responsibility—you do not have to judge anybody."

It has taken me years to really *hear* that wonderful revelation. Yet how glorious it is when it really comes into consciousness. The human mind so easily hurt, so easily offended, so easily set at war with its brother cannot accept such a lovely solution to all its problems.

"Vengeance is mine; I will repay" sounds like the words of a terrible God of the heathens, yet it is the lovely revelation of our own God.

A ball thrown against a wall will return with the same force it is thrown. The ugliness of the human mind will return to the sender without any effort on his part. If you are filled with human belief, the ugliness sent forth easily penetrates the so-called wall and produces a problem.

You do not have to judge. The judgment is already made before the act is committed. The moment you enter into any dealings with your fellow man, you have set an unseen picture into manifestation. In the interim, if you try to intercede the fulfillment with your human dishonesty, you will find in the final analysis that "vengeance is mine" has set in and you are required to pay to the utmost farthing, for we are moving with the law that "not one jot or tittle shall be removed until the law is fulfilled."

Amazing as it may seem, the *intent* of your action is what must and will be finally fulfilled. "In a way you know not of," the protection you have sought in legal or self-justification is as nothing. You will lay the full payment on the altar before you will bear away a blessing.

Without the Smell of Fire

Recently a person came to me with a note long since due. Out of the kindness of his heart, he had not presented it. This was perhaps wrong—we shall see. But the person who had accepted the loan in good faith took refuge (and what refuge) in the human protection that "it is outlawed by time—I do not owe it now." It is wonderful what the human mind can think up. But "the measure ye mete" stands like a terrible word. There is nothing to hide behind—you are naked and you are afraid.

Do you begin to understand why "vengeance is mine; I will repay" is such an important law? It is so wonderful, for it relieves you of all the getting even and the judging. You are told to "judge righteous judgment." That is the judgment of the Christ-Consciousness, the Presence. When this is recognized, the invisible light of Truth must and will come into being, and this coming into being may manifest itself as did the casting out of the seven devils—he may be as one dead. Do you begin to see how it is that the return of the ball from the wall will take care of itself? Are you afraid?

The wonder of it all is that the original contract must and will be fulfilled to the letter. The human mind thinks it has slipped through a technicality, but fundamentally the soul knows the intent and purpose of the contract, and it will be fulfilled. There is nothing to hide behind when the call comes, "Adam, where art thou?" Why do you hide? You are naked? The whole transaction is laid bare before the Power, and the fulfillment must and will take place if you are to stay in the Garden.

It is wonderful! We bless all those who curse us and do evil against us, for it is only another way for the Lord to come into His own power. Then what must happen to the human "protection"?

Vengeance Is Mine

"I was naked and I was afraid." You were afraid? Why? Because you sought out many inventions to hide behind, and all of them are nothing now.

Why this twisting and turning away from the original word you gave? Because of the worship of gold? The worship of money, the falling down to the power in matter? Well, now that you have it, what is to happen? It is wonderful! Now we are caught far afield, and now the "wise" human mind, or serpent, which had such clever advice has gone. Perhaps his head has been crushed. His tail may still be wagging, but his power is over. The temptation to believe in another power has had its day. The Lord thy God is *one* God.

The law of the human mind is "He that taketh the sword shall perish by the sword." He that taketh the human way of adroitness and cunning will perish by that selfsame way. There is no discount in the law of God. Your word (good, bad, or indifferent) shall not return unto you void, but shall accomplish whereunto it is sent. You knew when the word issued from your mouth what was the full and perfect intent of that word. No later interpretation of human rights or wrongs enters in. You knew, and that intent will and must be fulfilled. Where now are your battery of human ideas and opinions of dishonesty? You are afraid and alone, and you are naked—the *light* of revelation sees through.

"His rebuke was terrible," terrible because it exposed the dishonesty of the human mind and caused the fulfillment of this dishonesty to take place. It is wonderful! "Sit at my right hand, until I make thine enemies thy footstool" is not a gloating over some downcast one, but glorification in the cleansing of that soul. The devils, the "do evils" of that human consciousness, are being cast out. If he falls as one dead, he shall arise again, clean and ready to fulfill his word.

"My words are spirit, and they are truth," and they "shall not return unto me void but shall accomplish whereunto they are sent." They are sent into fulfillment, and they shall be fulfilled in their original and true meaning. Not one jot or tittle shall be removed until they are fulfilled.

Do you begin to see what you are relieved of when you know that "vengeance is mine" is an actual law of the universe going into action? "Adam, where art thou?" is the terrible call, and the cunning thing which has advised doesn't know what to say. "Adam, where art thou?" Answer.

The human mind thinks evil has escaped so long and has gotten by with its craftiness. It takes refuge in a cunning, dishonest intellect which advises, but the call "Adam, where art thou?" comes, and you are naked. All the facts are known of God, and you will fulfill to the last letter the contract.

"My words are spirit, and they are truth," and they "shall not return unto me void but shall accomplish whereunto they are sent." That is the wonderful revelation of your word. Would you have it any other way? Would you change a single thing about it? Even to the "every idle word shall be given account of?" No, not one change, for the word from your mouth is the word of Power and Light, and it shall accomplish all the wonders of Life. It is wonderful! "Speak the word."

Many are hypnotized with the letter, and many have said, "Well, I have spoken the word and nothing happened." Yes, exactly what you spoke happened—the fulfillment of your disbelief was made manifest. Just because you spoke the word of money when your consciousness was filled with poverty does not presage a downpour of substance to you. The measure (motive, intent) ye mete shall return unto you. Do you understand that it *shall* return, not perhaps or maybe it shall return? Do you begin to hear?

So you do not have to wreak vengeance on the one who has so dishonestly interpreted his word. His word will finally be fulfilled, and you in the meantime cannot lose anything by his dishonesty or his failure to fulfill. Do you begin to see your place of blessings and light? You "bless those that curse you," those who try, and apparently do, put over the evil interpretation, for this descent of Light upon them brings forth the truth of the situation. They must and will be relieved.

The perpetual question, "Why did this happen to me?" is answered in many ways. Why did the person you did so much for turn and rend you? Because you have no right to do so much for anybody if you are going to do it from the plane of sympathy instead of compassion. When you sympathize with anyone, you discount that soul's possibilities of being itself. Eventually the soul rises from this pigsty of human sympathy and goes unto its Father, just as you have done time and time again, and this rising upsets your applecart of sympathy. Why should he sit there any longer, receiving your recognition of his impotency and inability? Why should he look up to you instead of looking up to God? It all seems a little cruel, but you will understand. You are moving into the new dimension—the childish things of yesteryears are gone; they are nothing. This is the "meat for the strong man."

You can and will help many—not by going down to their level of belief, but by standing on the heights and permitting them the same privilege of arriving at the heights. It is glorious, this compassion and understanding of what they are going through, but not once do you descend to the level of "you poor thing." That only intensifies the situation by your agreement.

Yet can you "stand and see," and you will. It is wonderful. Praise the Lord, the word is being fulfilled, and even "the years that the locust hath eaten" shall be restored. All the unfulfilled contracts will suddenly begin to appear with their fulfillment. Strange as it may seem, you have never lost a thing. Do you begin to *feel-see* the revelation of the Lord omnipotent?

Then the chorus of voices: "Yes, but I bought stock in a bogus company;" "I saw all the lovely things I had done misrepresented;" "I heard wrong and terrible interpretations given to my words," etc. Yes, all this and more, but "vengeance is mine; I will repay" suddenly comes into being, and every wrong shall be adjusted, for now you are rising to the place where this mysterious power is natural instead of supernatural, and the fulfillment of even those things of yesteryear must and will take place. You will see it all "if you faint not," if you are not overcome again by the hypnotism of the human thought-pictures.

It is so wonderful when you know there is no retaliation on your part. You do not "give back as good as was sent"—you give back Light which will destroy the evil, and you are at peace. It is wonderful how your acts and words have been distorted to mean something which you did not intend. It is wonderful to see how the one you loved has been so loaded with poison from another as to turn and attempt to hurt you. It is all glorious, for it is all cleansing and purifying, and you have lost nothing. Stand and *see*, or else fall by the way of human belief.

"Yes, but she put out all this scandal about me; she tried to justify her ugly deeds by scandalizing me." Well, what of it? You are superior to all that. The parasite, when it is deprived of its blood, will turn and rend the thing upon which it was living, but presently it will find that not all its scandal and hatred has accomplished anything more than a return of these things unto itself. If you do not accept the lie, it must and will return to the sender and fulfill itself with accelerated force.

Yes, "vengeance is mine." You will see this lovely force of Light coming through and revealing freedom to the maniac in the tomb of human thoughts. It is wonderful! *I*—not you or some human thing—will repay. Can you set yourself and "see the salvation of the Lord"?

THE SECOND COMING

Then shall appear the sign of the Son of man in heaven ... and they shall see the Son of man coming in the clouds of heaven with power and great glory.

"Yet in my flesh shall I see God." The second coming of Christ is at hand. And yet it is as far away as it always has been. For those who have ears to hear what the Scriptures "say unto the churches" (temples, bodies), the new dispensation is at hand, this time right into the flesh—the union of Jesus (the body) and Christ (the Spirit) bringing forth the Flesh which is attuned to the new rate of manifestation and which will enable you to experience many new things. It is wonderful, for it is secret and hidden, and only those who see shall *see* just what it is that the Scriptures are saying unto the churches (temples—bodies).

The second coming, upon which the "second death" (the final physical death) shall have no effect, is again presented for those who have "eyes," for those who *believe* in the Word—not the words, but the *word* of the Christ.

This is the day when immortality in the flesh is possible or impossible, and if impossible, then it is right for the Christ-Consciousness to bring it into manifestation. Everything that is possible has been done as far as you are concerned; it is the *impossible* that is to be brought out. "Yet in my flesh shall I see God." Do you believe it, or do you want to argue about it all? Is it so? Or is Jesus Christ a liar? Until you can arrive at the premise that you stand alone, divorced from every man, woman, organization, or book, you cannot "enter into the Holy of Holies," the *consciousness* of the Presence here and now.

The Second Coming

First comes the recognition of the teachings of Jesus Christ. Do you believe that the land into which you are to enter is actually in existence, just as you believe that the picture you took is on the film, even though you cannot see it before it is developed? It is essential that you *believe* that the consciousness you are trying to bring out actually and literally exists before it is humanly possible for the materialization of it to take place. Even after you accept this state of things, it is not yet done. It is necessary for you to have the courage to enter in and become one with it, seeing no sign.

"Go in and possess the land" requires that you first recognize the *land* (consciousness) as a finished and completed manifestation in the invisible, and then that you have the authority to enter in and *possess* the land, consciousness. You may be able to do all this symbolically, but are you able literally to enter in? Are you able to move into the place of "He made himself as God" and accept your authority to "go in and possess the land?" This you must answer for yourself.

The second coming is to be a material thing, for it is to be a completion of the work of Jesus, a fulfillment of the power. Yet in *my* flesh (not somebody else's, but mine) shall I (not another) *see* God. In the temple, or body, raised to the spiritual concept of flesh, shall you see this power, for it is only through this body-temple that you can and will *step down into manifestation* all the things that are to come into your kingdom.

For instance, this (yet to you invisible) book must be recognized by me as finished and completed. Without this recognition, I cannot step it down through the temple-body and make it real. Otherwise, it would remain a book in the symbolical world, an unborn child, as it were. So presently you will come to the place of realization that *through your temple-body must appear all that is to do with your heaven-on-earth manifestation.* This is perhaps the hardest step to take, for the human mind has failed so ignominiously in its attempts to do things that it has become self-conscious instead of Self-conscious.

Until you conceive, perceive, accept, and appropriate the fact, literally and actually, that your body-temple, John Smith, is the place or manifest point in consciousness where the things that concern you must be stepped down into visibility, all the teaching of Jesus is in vain. The union of the body and soul makes this possible; otherwise, you have only symbolical manifestation—unborn children. All the desires of your heart are crying out for bodies, crying out to be born, and you have laid them away in the perfumed memories of human thought. "Awake thou that sleepest, and Christ shall give thee light."

Your body-temple is the place of "stepping down" the manifestation to a point of visibility. As the spiritual, permanent thing moves towards materialization, even as this book is now moving into reality out of the unseen, you suddenly realize the wonder of it all. Until you realize this, you continue to move about in a world filled with evil manifestations and chance. *There is no chance in the divine plan.* Chance exists only in the human consciousness because it has pairs of opposites, two powers eternally warring with each other.

The "losing your life" means the finding of your Life. It is a breaking of the small, limited pattern of the human consciousness. If you are still thinking to glorify the "John Smith," you will be defeated; your power will be for the moment, as the green bay tree which flourishes gloriously and then is suddenly withered away.

You are the dispenser of the revelation—you are the revelator.

The second coming is so wonderful and glorious. Nothing matters now, and yet somehow or other, every-

The Second Coming

thing matters. You can go in and possess the land because you are no longer working "miracles" but are actually *recognizing the Word* as It issues forth from the mouth of God. It is wonderful.

"For as the lightning cometh out of the east, and shineth even unto the west, so shall also the coming of the Son of man be."

Do you begin to see that the coming of the "second coming" is entirely beyond the human idea of time or space? Have you ever thought of a flash of lightning from the east to the west? Well, if not, think of it for a moment and then see how quickly the Spirit can come into manifestation in your life.

So is it with the Word (not words) spoken from this revelation of consciousness. It is like the lightning that in an instant flashes across the horizon and lights up everything. Do you begin to see what *your* word is? Or do you believe? Remember, the words of Master Jesus were: "The works that I do ye shall do also, and even greater works than these shall ye do." It is wonderful, isn't it?

Now you *must* be about your Father's business, which is so much greater than the business of John Smith, yet which suddenly picks up the limitations of John Smith and frees them into something glorious. It is wonderful, the quickening of the power which causes the manifestation to be stepped up into the fulfillment of what it is doing. Do you hear what *I* am saying unto you—or do you hear? Who are you? And when will you begin to accept *your* birthright?

Do you know that you were made in the image and likeness of God? Or do you? And if so, what will happen to this poor old human image of John Smith? Suddenly the life force will rush into manifestation and fill full the measure of your *true* Self, and the age and limitations of John Smith will be wiped out. Do you *see*? But not, of

Without the Smell of Fire

course, to prove to others that you have a power they know not of. What do you care what they think or try to prove?

"Behold, I come quickly; and my reward is (right) with me." Do you believe? Or do you? Right with Me. *I come quickly*—do you hear? In the darkest, most chaotic condition in your life, *I*, the *I* (blended Spirit and matter, Jesus Christ) come quickly into manifestation, and it is so.

> For as in the days that were before the flood they were eating and drinking, marrying and giving in marriage, until the day Noah entered into the ark, and knew not until the flood came, and took them all away; so shall also the coming of the Son of man be.

So shall also the coming of the Son of *man*-ifestation be.

Note that the old human so-called scientific mind continues with its thousand and one proofs of life. But the floods come. In your ark, in this new consciousness, will you sail away over the whole lot of human testimony which has bound you for so long, and in that ark, consciousness, you will have taken all that matters. It is wonderful! You are performing the Noah drama—building the ark and taking therein all that matters and then drowning out all that doesn't matter, along with the entire history of your case.

Do you hear, or is there something you want to retain from it all? Is there something you wish to carry over? You must answer, for in this ark (consciousness) you are taking over only that which is productive of increase and newness, a something that is to populate a new universe. Your universe! And with the sailing of that ark, all of the former things have passed away—the age, the history of your case, the fears, and the mistakes. You are actually a new creature in Christ Jesus.

It is wonderful—and if you read further, you will understand that the ark had only one window and that was straight up. No looking to the right or left or the past or anything that had gone before—it was only looking to the new dimension. It is wonderful! Or is it?

"Heaven and earth shall pass away, but my word shall not pass away." *You are the Word*, and no matter what you have put yourself through, you shall not pass away. Do you hear? When will you awaken to this permanent Identity, the Fatherhood degree?

Silence will come to you, the real silence. "Then shall two be in the field, the one shall be taken and the other remain." Do you begin to understand the silence? It is the same thing which covers the situation of "ten thousand shall fall at thy right hand, but it shall not come nigh thee." Be still and pass through. You cannot prove anything, because when you try to prove it for the curious, you fail. But you have to "prove me, and see if I will not open windows in heaven and pour out a blessing you will not be able to receive." It is all so paradoxical; you must not prove, in order that you *can* prove. One proving is from the standpoint of doubt, the other a fulfillment.

Keep silent—keep silent, for it makes no difference if the man you are working with or the manifestation you are in is not taken or is taken. Do you see? "Two women shall be grinding at the mill, the one shall be taken and the other remain." There are lots of women grinding at the mill; one may be grinding with you, but you may be taken and she may remain, even if she is your best friend, your mother, father, brother, daughter. Do you *see*?

You may be taken into the new consciousness, and then will you be silent and secret, yet *you will withhold from no man*. You can and will give to any man whatsoever he asks of you, but this time you have the *proper interpretation* of what he is asking. So you will give sometimes by withholding that for which he is asking. It is wonderful. You are through with all the outward show, for you have found the Christ-Consciousness and you are the temple of the living God, stepping down into visibility the things that were formerly dreams and imagination.

Praise the Lord. It is wonderful! Can you pause for a moment in your glorious revelation and recognize that wonderful one who discovered the Allness of Life and gave it unto you?

"Therefore be ye also ready, for in such an hour as ye think not, the Son of *man*-ifestation cometh." It is wonderful, this readiness, this willingness to lose your life and find it. To lose (loose) the limitations of John Smith and find the infinite capacities of life in Christ Jesus. *I write this unto you.*

"Blessed is the servant, whom his lord, when he cometh, shall find waiting."

Are you waiting? Are you in the consciousness which knows that it is so, and consequently are quietly waiting for the Lord to come into full manifestation? Wonderful, isn't it?

The glorious second coming of Jesus Christ is here for you—that is, if you hear it. It must be heard before you will open the door and let Him in to sup with you and to break the substance with you. It is *here*, now and completely, when you recognize that your body, even John Smith, is the temple of the living God.

Such a deep welling up of praise and glorification of the power comes over you when you are willing to let go of everything and follow Me.

"Who then is a faithful and wise servant, whom his lord hath made ruler over his household, to give them meat in due season?"

Are you the faithful servant, or are you still the silly Adam—John Smith—who tasted of the fruit of separation? You have to answer all this for yourself—not for you and another, but for yourself. Are you the faithful servant, the ruler over the *household*, or are you the little thing which is still trying to glorify John Smith, who has his seventy years and then death? You have to choose, and you have to recognize the principle back of your choice.

Who are you? Answer for yourself to yourself—no one else cares. "Verily I say unto you, that he shall make him ruler over all his goods."

Do you hear? If you are the temple servant of the universal God-power, you shall be made the ruler over "all his goods." Is all enough? Or do you need more? Is it more rent, more health, more life—more something that you need? What do you need? Could it be you need more God? You answer. The second coming is at hand.

PUTTING ON THE VESTMENTS OF YOUR OFFICE

THE WAY

The Jesus Christ Consciousness is the way, the truth, and the Light. There is no other way to enter into the kingdom of heaven but through Me. "No man comes unto the Father but by me." No man attains his Fatherhood degree but through the putting on of the Jesus Christ Consciousness. No one can reach the Fatherhood degree through Jesus ("I can of mine own self do nothing"). Neither can any man reach the manifest Fatherhood degree through the Christ, the Spirit. It must be the consciousness of Jesus Christ—Spirit materialized and matter spiritualized. In other words, a full recognition of the Flesh, in which you are to see God; a full acceptance that you have resurrected yourself into the consciousness of Spirit-matter, the perfect link between the unseen and the seen.

Jesus is helpless to do anything, and the Christ remains invisible. The two blending into one bring forth the Flesh. "Yet in my flesh shall I see God." It is a consciousness of God in the Flesh. "He made himself as God"—not God, but *as* God, of the same nature and substance, embodied in a temple through which the invisible decrees of God could take form and shape.

This consciousness, this recognition of your own Divinity, is putting on the vestments of your office. Daring to make the assumption that what Jesus said was true and real, and acting upon his invitation, "Go thou and do likewise," is the great step in the direction of fulfillment— heaven on earth. It is wonderful! "Be not afraid, it is I."

THE SECRECY

Once you have discovered this principle, you are suddenly made aware of the need of secrecy. "See that you tell no man," and if you have thought secrecy was important before, now you will be so aware of its importance that the coal of fire will be instantly clapped on your lips, for this is too precious to be cast unto dogs. No one believed Jesus; why do you expect anyone to believe you? "Be still, and know that I am God." Keep silent before Me. "Then went he in and shut the door." Your contemplation in silence will suddenly become something so wonderful as to be too precious to mention to anyone. But the Light that will emanate from your silence will speak for Itself.

IT IS CONSUMMATED

From now on, if you have anything to be performed in the physical, you will enter first into the silence and complete the recognition of its consummation there, then return unto the place of performance and go through whatever mechanics are necessary to bring it into manifestation—with this one difference, however: you will find the physical task falling to pieces. What seemed difficult will melt into ease. In fact, by the vision you have gained within, you will see it minimized before your eyes by a way "ye know not of."

IMPORTANCE

The importance of anything you have to do is entirely taken away from the situation, thereby taking away the possibility of stage fright, fear, inability, etc., for the whole thing you are to do has already been perfectly done in the consciousness of God. Your body is merely going through the mechanics of the work. You are about your

Father's (Fatherhood) business and all is perfect—not because you affirm that, but because you *know* it.

DIVINE INDIFFERENCE

This new dimension of working by the way of God first and following through by the way of man causes you to appreciate the *divine indifference* of God. You can be divinely indifferent because you are not doing anything of yourself as a man. You are operating and operated by Light.

POWER OF LIGHT

When you make the substitution of Light for the old human sense of power, you will begin to experience the fatigueless body. Instead of so much health functioning in your body, you will suddenly find you are propelled by Light. Light passing through your body does not exhaust strength or power. It is not used up. It is not under the limited concept of human strength. It functions perfectly at a moment you are absent from the body (the human sense of strength or lack of it). Hence, you may "run and not be weary."

Do you understand that this is an utter impossibility to the human man? Yet you shall run and not be weary. You shall eventually see how it is that Spirit has a fatigueless body, and making so many physical motions is not, as you have thought, the basis of gaining your living. The gaining of your living "by the sweat of your brow" ceases to have any meaning. You are fed, sustained, and held into place (no matter however impossible it may seem to the thought-man) by Light—the spiritual counterpart of the human belief in power. "Let there be light, and there was light." You are also told. "Let your light so shine." Do you hear? *Your* light. Do you begin to understand how it is that in an instant a body worn out with

Putting on the Vestments of Your Office

human fatigue can be rehabilitated and made strong, or a body worn away with the futility of disease can, through the passage of Light into place, become "every whit whole"?

The universe run by Light is the kingdom of heaven, for Light is the power which is above all human thought power. Throwing this Light onto a situation proves hell to be heaven and evil to be good. All this is part of your new Fatherhood business. It is wonderful! It is sacred and holy. Do not profane this name-nature by chatter of and about it. Keep silent before Me.

The so-called miracles of Jesus were all performed first in the place of Light. "Thank you, Father, I knew this was done." The full recognition took place, and then the Light, revelation, shone through the dense, opaque human belief and destroyed the appearances of lack, the Light penetrating everything. The invisible Light going through the stone wall, the prison cell, to the other end of the Earth suddenly becomes visible at the other end of the equation. Nothing can withhold It, nothing can stop It—it is wonderful.

Jesus, like you, is the "stepper-down" of the Light, the place where the invisible becomes visible.

By identifying yourself with this Light, you begin to experience things that to the human mind are fantastic. Jesus "passed through the crowds" and was instantly on the other side of the lake. So you see how the Light operates beyond the dimension of the human comprehension. But just as surely as you find yourself in a crowd of thoughts which are not desirable, you can also move through the crowd, and if you must have distance, you are at the other side of the lake. It is wonderful!

Do you begin to sense the power of this invisible Light? Evil in its most intelligent form does not suspect nor yet grasp the fact of Its presence until, "in the twinkling of an eye," It comes into manifestation, and no one has been aware that It was present. You are the possessor of the invisible Light which you can make visible by *letting* it into expression.

VALUE

In the New Day, nothing has any value; all is the manifest or unmanifest substance of God. The human mind places value on a thing until that thing reaches a point of saturation, and then the value goes, but the thing remains the same. Examine into the pearl market. The stupid human mind admits that the cultured pearl is so perfect that it is impossible to tell it from the so-called real one, yet because it is simpler and more easy of attainment, it has small value—but it has also taken most of the value away from the real pearl. "The wisdom of man is foolishness in the eyes of God," and do you wonder?

Remember this when next you desire to bring out something. Take first from it all the man-made value. This takes away much of the difficulty in getting it. The only value it has is in God, and you are *there*. Do you begin to see? If you want it, take it—but do not make it valuable.

GRAVITY OF HUMAN THOUGHT

Human thought is the source and center of all gravity. The more contemplation you give a thing from the human standpoint the heavier it gets and the more important. A horse can be trained to be so sensitive that it catches cold as easily as an infant. A trivial mishap or sin can be magnified into a mountain of difficulty. "Be absent from the body and present with the Lord" has a good reason, then. "Watch, and again I say, watch."

"MY WAY IS EASY AND MY BURDEN IS LIGHT"

The only burden you have is Light, in both nature and substance, and so you begin to understand something of the *new day*, which is even at this moment dawning before you.

CLOTHED BY SPIRIT

You are clothed by Spirit when you once recognize this "Flesh" body, and henceforth the Light becoming visible takes the form of suitable and proper clothing for you. Do you understand this? What you perform in the place of "it is consummated" will be made visible to the eyes. "Your heavenly Father (Divinity) knoweth ye have need of these things." It is all right. Are you afraid?

FED BY SPIRIT

You are fed and sustained by the Spirit. "Your fathers did eat manna in the wilderness and are dead," but you have bread they knew not of. "Man shall not live by bread alone, but by every word that proceedeth out of the mouth of God."

Isn't it wonderful! You shall never want for food again. You shall be fed. You shall take your place at the banquet table with the fatted calf. "If you had asked me, I would have given you the living waters, which if a man drinketh thereof he shall never thirst again." Are you thirsty? Why don't you ask Me, believing you have already received? It is wonderful!

"NEITHER DO I CONDEMN THEE"

Mary Magdalene is about to be stoned to death. She is taken to the wall of the city, followed by a mob of accusers. Then something happens.

Everybody sooner or later comes to the walls of his present consciousness, and if he does not get outside of it, he is stoned to death by his accusers. The sick man finally comes to the limits of his consciousness of sickness. It either takes him off—he is stoned to death by the accusing thoughts and beliefs—or else he goes beyond the walls of that state of consciousness into another level and suddenly he finds himself free from his accusers.

The inhabitants of your consciousness are the impersonated beliefs of your own mind. If you know a thing to be incurable, so does your entire world or city—state—and those very ideas and recognitions will embody themselves into witnesses against you.

As soon as the thought is broken about a given consciousness, the whole setup of that consciousness disappears with it. "Neither do I condemn you" causes one to look and see there are no accusers. The moment you are through with a thing in consciousness and let it go, it has gone from the only place it ever existed; the place thereof is no more, and it shall not come into mind (of anybody) anymore—that is, if you have broken it in your own mind. The moment you see this, "there is now therefore no condemnation in those who are in Christ Jesus."

It is so simple and yet so difficult, for in your human approach to the situation, you have a forgiven harlot or a cured sick man or a reformed drunkard or thief. But when you enter into the new consciousness, you find none of these things true. What you find in the new consciousness has always been true; you have merely come a step closer to the light and have more light. You do not get rid of anything; you become aware of more light. Hence, we do not come under the idea of a cured man or a redeemed harlot or thief, but we come to a consciousness, even in a degree, of the command "ye must be born again." If you are born again, even into a new state of consciousness of a limited degree, the limitations of the former thing are passed away and all things become new—or are discovered to be new.

In a dozen different ways, Jesus advised the *new* consciousness, the entering into the Christ-Consciousness which is the heritage of every man. Put not new wine into old bottles, new patches onto old clothes, else all is lost. So we are not pouring a little healing balm or forgiveness into the old carcass of sin and disease. You must be born again. You are not to be healed, but that which takes place is the releasing of consciousness—the new consciousness you suddenly recognize as a reality.

"Behold, I make all things new." The holier-than-thou consciousness feels righteous because it has reformed someone, but in the background it always retains the fact that it is an ex-something or other—an ex-sick man, an ex-convict, an ex-thief or something—and it feels so "spiritual" over having been instrumental in this overcoming. All this spiritual wickedness must go. The "born again" does not partake of the evil of the past state any more than the water lily partakes of the slime through which it has passed. "You are a new creature in Christ Jesus." All things are made new—and so it is.

"There is now no condemnation to those who are in Christ Jesus." There is no memory if there is no condemnation, for "the former things have passed away," and they shall not come into mind anymore. If they are out of your mind, they are out of the mind of everybody else, and you find you have no accusers.

It is wonderful when you see how the Power is constantly leading you back to your own Self, your Divinity, which was created in the image and likeness of God—a little lower than the angels—having dominion. Suddenly you are beginning to actually know that this perfect creation could not be dragged through the petty sins and sicknesses of the human thought formations. It is wonderful how this eternal, changeless You shines forth in the darkness of human thought, cancels the pictures of this congested thought and suddenly causes the harlot to be a virgin, for in the new consciousness into which she enters, there is nothing there of the former self and there is no condemnation—none of the acts, thoughts, or fears of the former thing remains.

So great is this transformation, this entering into the new state, that many times the fashion of the countenance is changed. "Is this the Magdalene?" Well, don't you know? Weren't you one of the accusers? Did you see her about, committing adultery—which you were so familiar with, in thought if not in body? You were one of the accusers, and you cannot even tell whether it is she or not. No wonder the confusion of the scandalmonger who, by the way, is the last thing that is to enter heaven. Harlots, liars, murderers, thieves, and all else finally go into the kingdom of heaven before the scandalmonger. What are your chances of getting into heaven? Watch.

If there is no condemnation in your life, there will be no stone casters. This is a hard lesson, for most of us reserve a few stones, covered with some kind of velvet or fur—"I don't want to say anything, but"—which we occasionally take out and cast. But presently we will *see*, and lo, there are no accusers. The former things are passed away.

"Neither Do I Condemn Thee"

"Is this the Nazarene?" Well, don't you know? What has happened when Jesus enters into a new consciousness? It seems as though he is secure from you and your stones since you are not certain who it is.

"Is this the cripple who sat at the temple gate forty years?" You are not quite certain, are you? This one you see is leaping and praising God, and the one you condemned or condoned or held in his place with your sickly sympathy was crippled, helpless, and sometimes you gave him a copper and went away feeling grand and noble.

Then suddenly you find you have arrived at the walls of your present city, consciousness, and after you, are a herd of your erstwhile fellow citizens ready and willing to stone you to death. You have tuberculosis—incurable. A thousand cases and testimonies rise up; row after row of them stand with accusing fingers. They have driven you to the wall of your consciousness.

Either break this thought and enter into the pure consciousness of Jesus Christ, or be stoned to death by your beliefs. And suddenly you *see*—you call and He answers, and then you find no one has cast a stone and you cannot find any accusers, for all of a sudden you are in a new consciousness which never knew anything about tuberculosis. Wonderful, isn't it—all your petty evils are the same, and so you can enter into the Lord and be at peace anytime you want to. It is glorious. We are in a new day, on the other side of the cross of crucifixion, entering into the facts of Life here and *now*.

"Where are your accusers?"

"Lord, no man accuses me."

"Well, neither do I." Go and see that you do not commit sickness or anything else again—no, not even poverty. Do you hear?

THE PATTERN

Instead of trying to change the shape of air in a room, we change the shape of the room, and the air immediately, or actually, is there before we do it. Before the unseen plans of the architect are made manifest, the place of the house is already filled with air. "Before you ask, I will answer, and while you are speaking, I will give it unto you."

The old idea of building a shape or a new consciousness which is a perfect vacuum and then filling it with air is the way of the human thought. The way of man is always from the outside in—the way of God is from the inside out.

"Put not new wine in old bottles, new patches on old garments" is the law. We are not trying anymore to change an old consciousness or patch up an old state of affairs. "You must be born again" is not primarily a physical demand—it is a breaking of the old pattern and an introduction of the new. A pint cup will hold only a pint, no matter into what shape you bend it and how long you work with it. If you want more, you will have to get a new pattern or matrix. A thousand barrels of water poured into a pint cup only nets a pint of substance to the owner of the cup. So the whole of God-substance could be poured over the consciousness of John Smith, and he would have no more than the pattern of his consciousness.

No wonder, then, the command, "Enlarge the borders of your tent," "Launch out into deep waters." If you want more, need more, and must have more than you have now, you will have to have a larger measure of it all—a larger consciousness of it.

This is not nearly so difficult as it appears from these words. The rule is well-stated by Jesus Christ: "Then went he in and shut the door." He suddenly closes the door of human thought and begins to contemplate the law, "Be still, and know that I am God," and as he begins to sense in a degree the infinite nature of God, he begins to appropriate the new design, matrix, or consciousness. In the language of Jesus Christ, "whatsoever you tell the Father (within) in secret, that will be called from the housetops." That is, whatsoever you can accept as true of this God-Consciousness will take the form of the new pattern.

Whenever you close your contact with the universal Whole, God, the air (life) becomes stagnant and dangerous. Health shut up in a body is bound to deteriorate, but once the consciousness of Life is even touched upon, the constant refreshing, renewing power passes through the temple, and all is well.

All of these illustrations are inadequate to express the idea of Jesus Christ, but they will in some meager way give light to guide you into the further day of Self-expression.

Gradually God will become more natural, and the supernatural quality will be absorbed. As your human intelligence blends with the Divine, you begin to draw on the intuitional and inspirational quality of God and see these things active in your life. It is wonderful and it is so, no matter what the appearances.

Eventually you will see that your body-temple is here for the expression of something bigger than what you have formerly called "you." There is a power bigger than all the beliefs you have accumulated in life. There is a power which can and will set aside all the beliefs of mankind—and it is that power, that Life, which Jesus recognized as being everywhere present.

As the wind passes through the screen, eventually you will experience Life passing through your body, cleansing it of everything that maketh a lie—everything that has a belief in human power as opposed to God. Do you begin to see that we are not curing the sick body but appropriating a new consciousness within, even though the appearances are all against it? We go within and take the new concept of health and life, though there is no evidence of it without, and the substance will fill the new design and make itself manifest without effort. Eventually you will see it in the flesh, for it is already there in the invisible before you ask.

As the walls of the room go into place, the air inside gradually takes shape. As the consciousness of the new idea takes place, the manifestation begins to appear, for the substance is already there. "Now faith is the substance of things hoped for, the evidence of things not seen." Faith that is *recognition* of the Presence of God here, there, and everywhere is the substance, just as the air exists before the shape of the room is made. It is the very evidence of things not seen, but which are there.

You hold the shape of the air in the room as long as you keep the room in place, and this goes for everything–good, bad, or indifferent. As long as we hold the consciousness of evil, sin, and sickness, we have it filled with the human thought-substance of these things. But the moment the walls of the room are torn down, then there is no shape to the air inside.

"Ask, believing that you receive, and it shall be so." This asking is not beseeching or trying to make God do your bidding. It is a glorious relaxation, a sort of sudden recognition of "Behold, I (this consciousness) stand at the door, and knock: if any man hear my voice, and open the door, I will come in to him, and will sup with him, and he with me."

Do you begin to *hear*, in the new way, that the purpose of your existence here is for the God-power to express? I know we have all been far afield, caught in a thousand and one beliefs of race consciousness and human hypnotism, but now we are arising from the pigsty of human thinking and moving towards the Father-Consciousness. It all seems so difficult when we think about it, yet so simple when we still the conscious-thinking and *let* this glorious power come into manifestation by "I have a way ye know not of." The moment we do the thing by the way of God—go within and accept this Presence—then we will do it by the way of man—we will see it in the flesh.

"Put up your sword." "Set yourselves and see the salvation of the Lord" is something that must and will take place. When you put up the sword of human thought, the fighting of conflicting opinions and beliefs will disappear, and you will see the salvation of the Lord. And presently, in this lovely relaxation of the Presence, your Life will be one lovely recognition of "My Lord and my God"—the Presence here and now with you.

THE HOST

"He made himself as God." He entered into the Fatherhood degree and became the Host, the point through which flowed the unseen substance into manifestation.

We see Jesus standing on the level of five thousand hungry men, with nothing to give them but five loaves and two fishes, which would have fed half a dozen or so people. That is the actual fact by all consensus of opinion and by the findings of the best human intellect.

When Jesus—on that plane of consciousness—starts to break five loaves of bread, he naturally decreases the size of the loaves. This we all acknowledge, and if he remains on that plane of consciousness, he has all the race consciousness to back him up. The five thousand hungry men knew there was nothing and knew they were hungry, and that was the truth on that level of thinking.

Had Jesus remained on this level, he would also have experienced hunger and lack and the problems ensuing therefrom. But he went unto his Father (the mind which was also in Christ Jesus and which is in you), and at that level he becomes the eternal Host. In the consciousness of the All, the slow process of planting, cultivating, harvesting, milling, baking has nothing to do with it, for the flower is found before the seed, and there is no man to till the soil and no rain. In other words, when he makes the assumption of his God-given heritage, he perceives the "substance of things hoped for and the evidence of things not seen." In this place, he becomes the Host and can break the bread to increase instead of decrease, for he is touching the unseen and the seen, and the endless flow of substance through the visible point increases instead of decreases.

The moment the human thought tries to handle this eternal Host, with its increasing substance, the idea turns to dust and becomes nothing but a theory as full of holes as a net. "Who can know the mind of God?" Certainly not the foreshortened human thought which is "a liar and the father of it."

The human thought consciousness is never a giver, but an eternal getter. He cannot conceive of letting himself be a channel through which substance could pour into expression unless that substance ran into his private granaries. The human consciousness may demand a loaf; he will take a half. Failing in this, he will take a slice and has been known to go under the table with the dogs for crumbs. Hence, the impossibility of approaching this Host state through thought. It is a recognition of the Presence and the acceptance of the capacity of man "made in the image and likeness of God" which steps this invisible substance down into manifestation and actually causes the precipitation or increase of substance to take place.

Thought cannot touch this state of consciousness, for it cannot "believe." In fact, it is a complete reversal of everything man knows and accepts as the Truth. Hence, "the wisdom of man is foolishness in the eyes of God" holds more than true here in this Host degree of understanding. Yet with the mightiness of it all, with all the miraculous appearances, the simple Jesus said to those hungry ones the next day when they still sought for bread: "What? You did not see the miracle—the power—the revelation? You saw only the bread?"

This assumption of the Host is not a mystical play of words or a psychic manifestation; neither is it an emotional episode. It is assumption of your heritage which is above all thinking. It has to be *accepted*, for no amount of thinking could in any way figure it out. It is the same thing which happens when a man born blind is asked, "Will you receive your sight?" Remember that he has never had sight, so if he starts to think about it, he is lost at the outset. He doesn't even know what sight is, and he has no eyeballs. Yet in the illustration given, the answer is "Yes." The recognition of this capacity on the spiritual plane causes the human thing to instantly catch up with the decree of Spirit, just as the "look again" causes the fields to be white with harvest. Yet the laborers are few—few people there be who want to be aroused from this sluggish human thinking, because it disturbs all the old human beliefs. "Why have you come here to disturb us?"

    After the miracle of the loaves and the fishes, many returned again to Jesus for bread and fish, but they could not find him. "You seek me after the loaves and fishes, but you cannot find me." That is, they could not again come into the presence of the Host degree of power.

    The increase of substance is one of the powers of the Host. The moment you become conscious of this capacity, you will begin to see things happen of which you have only heard before. You will experience the facts of Jesus' teaching that whoever makes the assumption of the Host consciousness finds enough and to spare, literally as well as figuratively, at any table to which he sits.

    It is too good to be true, but it is true. It cannot be proven by the curious, but it can and will be done if the occasion demands. Remember always the common sense of Jesus Christ. The morning after feeding five thousand, he asks, "Children, have you any meat?" It doesn't make any difference through which temple the manifestation comes—it can come through any temple that is called upon. The question in the human mind is why should Jesus have to ask for bread and fish when he could do such wonders? The answer is: "Ask, and ye shall receive," and the way and means of its appearance are of small moment.

None of this revelation is for "proof." If you are still trying to prove the truth, it is because you do not *believe* the Word and are trying to square it by the human reasoning. You will not be able to do so, and the simplicity of it will baffle you again and again, and you will ask, "Why doesn't it work for me?" Stop a moment—do you expect God Almighty to arrest the glorious Self-expression to prove anything to you?

When you align yourself with God, you will begin to see and hear and understand many things which already exist but which cannot be proven for the sake of proving them. There is too much doubt and questioning in the mind that is going to prove God to see whether it works or not. I can tell you now that it will not work—yet you are told to "prove me and see." That proof is merely the recognition of the Presence whenever you come into the place of need or lack. Sitting down to any table as the Host enables you to feed as many as come to that table by the subtle action of the Power, which breaks to increase and keeps passing the substance of Life from the unseen to the seen. But the moment prying eyes come into place, the whole thing is hidden behind a veil of human reasoning, and so nothing appears to be happening after all.

"The signs shall follow—they shall not precede." Do you hear? Do you believe?

Assuming your Host degree relieves you from the worry of the how and the where—or the possibility of it taking place. As many as called on Him were answered, and so you proceed to serve from the unseen to the seen. No language can explain this subtle idea, yet is it simple enough for the child.

Whenever you are through getting, you will "go in and possess the land," the consciousness, and find abundance and more than abundance there, ready and waiting to come into manifestation. Then will you turn the water into wine if necessary, and the best wine at that. Then will you break the bread and feed as many as come, if it be necessary. It is wonderful. Go down to the sea of Life and call up a fish (idea) and take from his mouth the piece of gold that Caesar wants. That will satisfy him and cause him to be at peace.

Lord of Lords and Host of Hosts. It is wonderful. Pause a moment in this holy capacity of the Host.

THE ECHO

The answer to real prayer is like the echo of a voice. It is automatic and instant. It is the materialization of the Word which has gone forth. There is no question about the results. "Before you ask, I will answer" takes care of that. The eternal substance of the thing asked for is always there, just as the acoustics are always there to cause the echo to take place. The echo is the materialization of the Voice—the agreement, the answer. The moment the Word is released, *it is done*. What follows is entirely outside of the power of the one speaking. The moment the prayer is made, *it is finished* so far as the prayer is concerned. The answer is entirely automatic, just as the echo, and nothing can be done about it.

The prayer, or the Word, which has its echo (manifestation) has little to do with the words of human thinking. There is only *one* Word, indivisible and eternal. There are millions of words in hundreds of languages, none of which are capable of accomplishing anything of great merit. "My word shall not return unto me void, but shall accomplish whereunto it is sent." This is the voice of pure recognition speaking, just as the person in a canyon could say with absolute certainty that his voice would return to him as an echo.

No illustration is adequate to bring anything but a faint impression of the power of God, but the *Word*, in contradistinction to the words, gives a certain something. Only speak the Word—not the words. Words, phrases, affirmations, and mantrams are as useless and incapable of obtaining results as the braying of a donkey. Yet the human mind persists in making long and wordy prayers or treatments, hoping to win the ear of God and cause Him to do something He would not otherwise have done.

There is no question about the answer to prayer that is made in accordance with the instructions of Jesus Christ: "When you pray, believe that you receive, and it shall be so"—this pure appropriation of the *it is done* consciousness which believes, actually and literally, that there is a God. Anyone will confess with his lips that he believes in God, but nine times out of ten he knows something called "problem" which has proven stronger than God, and it is for this reason he has come to pray and beg and beseech this God-thing to set aside the wrath of an apparently stronger power.

The prayer that is made from "it is done" consciousness takes off at the same easy level that the child does when he enters into his legend of Santa Claus. He accepts it. He cannot think it out, for it is not so on a *think* plane. Neither is the answer to prayer possible on a think plane. The moment you try to think that the prayer is answered before it is made, the intellect is so insulted that it simply dismisses the whole thing as impossible, and that is exactly what it is.

Everything you are seeking is impossible, or else you would have brought it forth long ago. Jesus was the doer of the impossible, not by overcoming the impossible but by the happy faculty of believing in God—believing in something greater than human thinking and its outpicturing. So he did not overcome—he entered into the consciousness of the *it is done before you ask*, without trying to analyze it on the three-dimensional plane of thinking. "Who by taking thought ...?" "Who can understand God?" No one can understand the infinite with the finite. The more he tries the more he runs into the age-old problem of the chicken and the egg and the egg and the chicken—which came first? He is up against a wall which he cannot scale.

"Answer before the asking" is impossible for the human mind to grasp. Jesus did not know how to solve that "impossibility" from the Jesus consciousness, for he exclaimed, "Of mine own self I can do nothing." But he did do precisely what the child did, and that was to appropriate, believe in God—believe and enter into the consciousness of the Christ—and in so doing, he found the impossible possible, the unseen seen, the unheard heard, and heaven on Earth, or in the midst of the human hell.

There is no explaining the supernatural which becomes natural as soon as it is accepted. Jesus entered into this Christ-Consciousness, which he discovered indigenous in every man, and functioned from that level. He found it natural to do those things which had formerly appeared supernatural, and possible to do those things which had been impossible. Hence, the *light* that comes to us from his revelation of the way of prayer.

"Believe, and thou shalt be saved." This is not a thought-taking process, filled with all the limitations of the world, but a definite recognition and acceptance of the Presence here, there, and everywhere. This consciousness can "look again" and see that which the sight of the human eye cannot even vision and the touch which can reach across the universe and release virtue and cause transformation.

It is wonderful when you see that you are through with the old idea that you are a "worm of the dust," busy trying to correct this fallacy or better the condition of the worm. The caterpillar crawls over every inch of the ground and dreams of flying, but he never can fly in that state of consciousness. Man crawls over every inch of his history and his problems and dreams of a freedom from pain and fear, but in the consciousness of the Adam-thinking he has nothing with which to take his freedom—*and until he can take it, he cannot take it.*

Any trying to prove God only results in the descent of the opaque curtain of human thought. You do not pray to find out whether God will do a thing or not; you pray the prayer of recognition and releasement. The automatic power that sets in to bring about the "echo" is entirely out of the mind of man. The moment it has gone forth, it is like the letter dropped into the post box—it is on its way, and the answer will return eventually. The carrier pigeon must be released if the reinforcements are to come up. Holding him by a string, no matter however long, and pulling him in every little while to see if he is all right will bring about disaster. So with the so-called prayer of the human thought. It constantly examines, questions, and doubts its words and eventually is self-annihilated.

In the consciousness of a problem, you cannot take the answer, just as the egg cannot fly yet at the same time being filled with the power to accomplish just that thing. The consciousness must be changed. The child cannot bring forth anything he does not accept without question, and neither can you. This reference to the child is in accordance with Jesus' teaching, indicating how simple and natural the whole thing is. It has nothing to do with childishness but a state that can *believe* without seeing or having it proven.

The change of consciousness is a poor way of indicating the appropriation of the Gift, but since there are few words to convey this revelation of Jesus Christ, we must apply them as best we can.

When the actual recognition of this inner Lord takes place in the consciousness of man, he suddenly rises. He suddenly sense-feels something beyond thinking. He is able to grasp a no-thinking state of recognition, a beholding as it were, where words and thoughts are superfluous

The Echo

and the consciousness is impressed with pure recognition that there is a God; a sensing of the substance of "my Lord and my God"—a heavenly contemplation of Life here and now, which the narrowing dimensions of thought cannot grasp with its measure of health and sickness, poverty and riches, happiness and wretchedness. There is the moment when he can say, "Thank you, Father," because he actually believes and sense-knows that it is so and that his Word is accomplished. He does not wait for the echo; he is not expectant of it. He is divinely indifferent to it all, for it automatically takes place. "Thank you, Father, I knew that this was done," yet did he say it because of the heavy thought-taking ignorance.

Jesus tried to show them the miracle; they heard only the *echo*. The next day they were looking for more echo, and there was no voice with which to create it or release it. Hence, man has sought God perpetually for results instead of for Cause and has failed to find his echo, because he could not accept the facts of his being. "Whatsoever you ask in my nature"—not in the nature of the present consciousness of problem, but in My nature, in the nature of your Christ. Not in the nature of the caterpillar but in the consciousness and the full acceptance of the butterfly. And once this acceptance is made, he enters into his cocoon and awaits the echo which says, "Come forth into manifestation," no matter whether this waiting be one instant or longer. The reward is always with the *word*, and the manifestation will take place at the exact moment it is necessary.

As the revelation of this glorious freedom dawns upon the hard-pinched consciousness of man, he begins to sense an inner warmth, a secret consciousness developing in him. It is like the hard kernel of popcorn on the heated stove—presently it bursts the shape or outline and spreads itself into a new and glorious manifestation. So the diseased consciousness suddenly lets go of the bondage of human thinking and comes out into its illimitable sense of life. From that new elevation, all things new are his, and an entirely different outlook on the whole universe takes place.

As the butterfly looks down upon his cocoon and the bird his egg, so man sees at last the limitations he has left behind him, sees them at that moment actually disintegrating and knows that presently they shall be no more, for they are gone, and the place thereof is also gone. It is wonderful how the mercy of God covers the Earth as the waters.

Presently man stops working with a problem and turns to the recognition of consciousness, the mind which was also in Christ Jesus, and feels the new consciousness spreading its wings for the new day of realization. A peace that passeth all understanding descends upon him, and he enters unconsciously into the paths of peace and harmony. He is not then constantly approaching the throne of God with a bag full of problems but with the recognition and the glory of it all.

As soon as the greedy human mind stops trying to get, it finds itself in the place of the giver and understands the overflowing chalice of God's love to man. It is wonderful to approach God with a clean mind, a mind free from the selfishness of trying to get something, and to enter into the heritage naturally and normally.

"Come boldly unto the throne of grace." "Come unto me, all ye that labor and are heavy laden, and I will give you rest." Come into this consciousness of God and speak the *word*. The echo "I will" will come back to you, and you will be at peace.

Even though you have faith or recognition as a grain of mustard, you shall say to yon mountain of problems "be thou removed, and be thou cast into the sea" of oblivion, and it shall be so, for the grain of mustard is multiplied a thousandfold when it is cast into the earth and allowed to come forth untrammeled by human thought. The film as small as a postage stamp is enlarged and thrown onto the screen a thousand times its original size by the light which penetrates it—so the prayer which is asked in this consciousness comes forth in manifestation a thousand times greater and more abundant than the idea in the mind of man.

The automatic power of the Light causes the manifestation to be more than you ask or think. The moment the consciousness is taken from the idea, it disappears with the same ease a picture disappears from the screen the moment the film is cut. This also applies to the film of human thought, which has been projected on your body and which has seemed so real and terrible. The moment the thought is broken, the manifestation is gone. In a mysterious way, the body is found perfect and normal—man is found sitting at the feet of the Master, in his right mind. He has suddenly arisen to his God-Self, and the body is thereafter a willing servant and not a separate intelligence.

Speak the word, and echo answers with sure and certain results, "I will," and the servant is healed in the same hour. Your *word* shall not pass away, neither shall it return unto you void. The ease of recognizing this will destroy the disease of human thinking.

Peace be unto you.

BUT HOW DID IT EVER HAPPEN?

However in the world, if we were created perfect and given dominion over everything, should we find ourselves in the awful confusion of evil?

Adam and Eve have been used as the type souls to see whether they could take the "all good" of life without question, without reason—in other words, whether they could take their good. Almost immediately we find a certain quality rising in them which is the final undoing of their kingdom. How many times have you thought of what a wonderful opportunity they had and wished you might be placed in a heaven—yes, even if it did have one restriction.

The one law that God holds over His universe is absolute obedience—no matter what the argument is. Without this obedience, this absolute control of the people of His universe, it would have fallen to pieces.

An old German story lends some light to the situation. It appears that once upon a time, a very rich and eccentric baron overheard two young married peasants talking in the garden under his window. They were discussing Adam and Eve and what fools they were for not having stayed in the Garden.

"Ah!" said the young girl, with a look of wonder in her cornflower blue eyes, "if we were only in the Garden and could live and enjoy life with no cares or worries, it would be wonderful."

"Yes," said her husband, "we would easily refrain from eating the fruit from the tree set aside for that purpose."

"Ah, yes, from a dozen trees, if only we could have had the chance to live in that paradise."

But How Did It Ever Happen?

By now the baron was interested, and going to the window, he called the young people into the house.

"I have decided," he said, "to give you your chance at heaven on Earth. I am going to take away all your work and give you the lovely cottage in the garden in which to live. Everything you desire will be given you, and you shall have servants to wait upon you. We shall see if you are any more capable than Adam and Eve."

Soon the young couple was installed in the beautiful little cottage. Every day their meals were served in elegant porcelain, silver, and crystal. All day long, they were free to do what their fancy pleased. They were very happy, until one morning the butler brought into the dining room a huge silver dish which had a heavy cover and placed it in the center of the table, saying to the young couple, "This cover is never to be removed."

"That is no matter," said the husband. "We have everything we want anyway, and why should we open the dish— what could possibly be in it, anyway?"

"Yes," agreed the wife, "we have everything, but I wonder why this is always to be placed on the table?"

"Well, never mind," said the husband, "only it would have been more sensible to have locked it up if we were not to open it, don't you think?"

"But," said the wife, "what on earth could it be? We have everything."

"I don't know and I don't care," said the husband. "We promised we would not touch it," running his fingers over the heavy cover. "It does not seem to be anything other than a large covered silver dish."

"That's just it," said the little wife, also tracing the heavy silver design over the top of the cover. "If it is just a plain dish and contains nothing, why should it be such a sin if we looked inside and had done with it?"

Frightened a little at her own daring, she backed away from the table. Her husband turned an angry glance upon her. "It is all foolishness—just a prank of that silly old man."

"Don't talk like that about the Baron; look what he has done for us."

"Well—"

"Well!"

"That stupid old butler is always bobbing in and out, anyway," said the little wife. She had come back to the table again and had slipped her hand in that of her husband as it rested near the handle of the dish. Suddenly she bent his fingers about the handle. He quickly drew back, and the butler came and removed the things from the table, all but the large silver dish, which remained there eternally.

At first the dish had only been noticed and remarked upon occasionally, but as time went on, more and more speculation was made as to its contents. Every sort of guess was hazarded. Still the great mystery. There sat the dish, apparently getting larger and more important each day, until at last it was all they thought or talked about.

And then one morning, after a long, sleepless night, the inevitable happened …

Once the cover was lifted, out flew a gaily colored bird and circled about the room and passed out the open window. The next morning the young couple were again in the fields earning their living by the sweat of their brows.

Curiosity is no part of Spirit. It is purely and simply one of the qualities of the human mind, and a very insidious one. The curiosity about the "how" of Spirit is so great that it has kept man from experiencing healing. He wants to open the Holy of Holies and see what is therein. Nothing of any importance is there once he has gotten it open, but much of unimportance has entered into his life. He suddenly finds himself "earning his living by

But How Did It Ever Happen?

the sweat of his brow" because he could not accept his good without opening the secret door. He could not come under the law of obedience. As the leper has said, "Are not Abana and Pharpar, rivers of Damascus, better than all the water of Israel?" Yes, they are, but that little something of obedience is so much more important, for it indicates the complete giving over of the human thought to the Divine—that is all.

"I have a way ye know not of," nor can you ever find out. Why, then, will you be so foolish as to try to reason out the way of God? Through your human consciousness, it is impossible for the things of Spirit to take place. So steeped in the history of the case, which in turn is backed up by thousands of years of proof that you are right, it is impossible to "see" how this is all nothing. If man could just get a look at God in action. "No man shall see my face and live," saith the Lord. Do you want to be the exception? Any man who sees the face of God dies instantly to all he formerly knew.

It is all so wonderful, this revelation, and how you will see that the "nothing" you want to see is actually nothing. Out of this great nothingness comes the everything. It is all so precious and so deep in its interpretation. Be still for a moment or two, will you, and let some of this lovely Light filter in; then you will not question, nor will you again "take thought" of the journey, scrip, purse—and find they are all supplied. And if you are told to do a thing, that thing will you do, not questioning how, why, when, or where. You will move forth by the power of Light, the God-thought substance. You will be operated by this Light and will receive tuition you have never dreamed of. You will find you are doing what you have to do—just right. No wonder it is all sacred and precious, and so holy *now*.

Without the Smell of Fire

Finally, "He shall give you the desires of your heart," in their highest and most perfect interpretation. Do you believe? Do not take off the cover of the silver dish. Do not open the seed. Do not profane the temple anymore. When you stretch forth your hand to steady the ark of another by your super-intellect or criticism, you suddenly find your arm withered away.

"O taste and see that the Lord is good." It is so wonderful! Beloved! You are able at last to "fold your tent and steal silently away," away into the new dimension. Nothing else matters; you have found your refuge. You have found your pastures where you may "go in and come out."

Get rid of the silly curiosity of the human mind, along with all the tricks of trying to prove God or trying to slip by unseen. Come out from among all these false ideas and enter into your heaven here and now. I am so glad you have found Him. All is well *now*. Do you hear? Do you believe? No matter what the appearances are? All is well.

The soul is incurious once it has touched the source of its being. It then becomes aware of all.

Once a student of truth went to India to study with a master. His first question to the master was, "Tell me how to become enormously rich, will you?"

"Yes," said the master, "all you have to do is go over to yon banyan tree, sit down, and meditate upon God. But during your meditation never think of a monkey, or else you will never be rich." The student hastened away. Quickly seating himself under the tree, he closed his eyes and attempted to think of God, but from that moment on, monkeys in increasing numbers roamed through his thoughts, until at last he found himself in a jungle filled with them.

If you are to bring forth substance, you cannot keep thinking of the symbol of substance. First must you put

But How Did It Ever Happen?

from you all such limitations, in order that the new measure may come into manifestation.

In every instance, the difficulty lies in the fact that man is trying to add substance to his unchanged consciousness, as if the caterpillar were to keep thinking about flying and trying to fly with the consciousness of a caterpillar. As soon as he recognizes this, he will make the consciousness fit the desire, and then he will fly. It is wonderful! So will you. Do you hear?

"When you pray, believe that you receive" so fills your mind that the out-picturing of the substance will take care of itself because the consciousness will begin pouring substance into manifestation through you.

THE POWER OF THE "LET THERE BE"

In the beginning—in the starting, as it were—there enters into the equation the speaking of the Word, the "Let there be."

And God said, "Let there be." With the ease, with the nonchalance, with the consciousness that it was possible, did he speak the Word—*let*. So small a word and yet so full of wonder and power. Spoken with the effortless, unlabored action of Mind.

In the command "let" there is hidden the possibility—yea, the infinite possibility—that it is so and can take place. A little later in the story, we hear the command "Let that mind be in you which was also in Christ Jesus."

The world is filled with people *trying* to "let," who make the most glorious failures on one side, the side of accomplishing good, and who make the most magnificent demonstrations of the power on the negative side.

The ease with which you catch disease is magnificent. I say magnificent, for without an effort you merely say, "I am catching cold," and you do. Without an effort you say, "I lost my job, I have poor health, I am going downhill," and a thousand and one things in the negative side of life prove in the reverse the law of "let there be."

Jesus said the human mind was a liar and the father of it. It therefore works perfectly in reverse and proves the law of the Presence in a manner which is alarming. "When I would do good, I do evil—amazing and yet interesting.

Hundreds of people say to me, "I cannot grasp the truth." They cannot and they do not see they are grasping the *law* of "let there be" in the reverse and functioning it

The Power of the "Let There Be"

perfectly. A "successful failure" is more than a play on words. To be a successful failure requires a reverse action of the law of God, and the reverse action of God is all that the human mind is capable of.

When man, in his own *free will*, decided to become a co-creator with God, he left the Edenic state of life and wandered into a labyrinth of human incarnations and beliefs, always imagining he could create something but always winding up with failure, disease, fear, poverty.

It is an easy thing for any human being to "commit" poverty. He finds it easier to lose a job than to keep one; easier to be diseased than at ease; easier to commit sin than to live in righteousness; and finally easier and more natural to commit war than peace. Always setting up a pair of opposites, good and evil warring against each other, there is no possibility for the human mind to ever attain peace as such. Jesus knew this well when he said, "I can of mine own self do nothing … but …"

Thousands of people are praying for release from evil of human thought, which is the only source of evil and the only sustainer of it. They pray "hard." They pray emotionally. They pray with all the might in their human minds, yet little happens. Nations pray for peace, but nothing happens because it is so difficult to have prayer answered—or so the human mind says. But on the other hand, it is very simple to have misfortune or sickness or poverty. Yes, it is easy because it is natural. Strange how long we have been in the place of the manifestation of thought and have not yet seen why evil manifested itself so much more easily than good.

"When you pray, believe that you receive." "Let that mind be in you which was also in Christ Jesus." *Let* is the stumbling block. You can easily "let" yourself catch cold. Why? Because you consciously know it is easy and natural and that you cannot stop it. All your human mind is in a perfect state of acceptance of it all. In other words, you are practicing the perfect law of prayer in reverse, and you are getting the exact results. And still you will not see that when you pray you have to have the same ease of letting the Word come through into manifestation. It should be as easy to catch good as it is to catch a cold.

Perhaps this all seems a little facetious to you. It is not meant to be. As soon as you can arrive at the place of the easy and natural acceptance of the Presence, you will see good manifested with the same assurance you see disease and evil. Do you begin to glimpse why prayer is not answered? It is because you try to "make" God do your bidding. You try to "make" demonstrations but *let* yourself catch cold. You are so saturated with the so-called truth of evil that it has the open ground and cooperation of everything, and it easily comes into manifestation.

"When you pray, believe that you receive." It does not say *make* yourself believe; it does not indicate credulity, hypnotism, or a lot of mental tricks. *Believe*—not make yourself believe. When you *let* on the positive side of life, you will not *make* or *try* to let, but you will see that fine distinction of *letting* with the same hopelessness that you let evil into manifestation. By recognition in the human mind of the power of evil, you have been educated to know that "as for man, his days are few and full of trouble," and you function on that basis until you begin to see and understand "what is the breadth, and length, and depth, and height" and majesty of God. Then you see why your prayers have not been answered.

Could you pray the *let* prayer of recognition, the speaking of the Word with the abandon of Jesus, you too would see the results just as naturally as you do in your evil dimension. The supernatural state of affairs has made it so impossible. You, a "natural," have been trying to use the supernatural.

The Power of the "Let There Be"

Jesus warned you against this, knowing that such prayer would be only emotion or fear or something other than Love. He said over and over again, "I can of mine own self do nothing." He was not foolish enough to think the human mind, undisciplined as it was and steeped in fear and hypnotism, could approach the supernatural. If he was to bring forth the reality of being, he would have to enter into that state of being where the supernatural becomes natural.

As soon as you go into a state of consciousness, you partake of that consciousness, and it then becomes natural and real. It ceases to be supernatural. So with the revelation of Jesus. He said, "I go unto my Father," a statement that has confused many because they have wanted to make something mystic out of it all; wanted to do something mysterious and strange with life. Yet with ease anytime, they could enter into the opposite realm of disease, fear, poverty, evil, accident and see it function with perfect success. It is so natural. God must finally be natural.

When you enter a warm room, you take on the temperature of that room. You do not make your body warm—it partakes of the nature, temperature, of that room. No miracle is performed. "If I be lifted up, I will draw all manifestation unto me" is quite natural, even though it be to man a miracle. Do you begin to see the state of mind one must be in, in order to bring out the Word made flesh? It must be as easy and as natural to bring forth good—to let God express in you—as it is to let a cold take possession of you.

When you pray (what a wonderful statement) what do you do? Begin to ask for a thousand and one things? Or do you go unto the Father within, the perfect Identity, and see what the picture that is forming on the face of the deep is to be for you? Remembering that your Father, your own Consciousness, knoweth that ye have need of all of these things, you do not need to bother with the forcing or asking or trying to cajole God into giving you something of which you stand in actual need.

"And God said, let the dry land appear." The impossible takes place—dry land out of wet water. How is that to happen? Try to reason that out. Is there anything in your human thinking that can produce a like phenomenon? Can you, by the widest reaches of human thought, take dry land out of wet water? It is impossible, but it can only be done by the *let* of God and not by any effort, belief, affirmation, or treatment—it must be on the plane of the *let*. Still, it is something to wonder at.

Can you see any difference in that equation and the one on which you are working? How can you let prosperity come out of poverty? How can you let health come from disease, harmony from inharmony, and order out of chaos—and yet you are "trying" to do all of these things. As long as you try, you are not going to do them; you are only going to intensify the problem. You will still seek for something on the outside that can help you, or a way in which you can introduce something into the picture which will cause the land to suddenly appear dry out of the water, but you will fail, for nothing on the outside can happen until it takes place on the inside. Whatever takes place within takes place in the without—and does not ask for permission or power to perform the so-called wonders.

No one can vaguely understand how you can take a well body out of a state of disease, chronic or acute, but it can be done by the *let*. No one can understand how a man in Job's fix, having lost everything—reputation, fortune, friends, and family—can suddenly have "twice as much as he had before" and have his captivity turned. It is not within the possibilities of man to understand that. "Who can understand the mind of God?" Answer that, and then you will stop trying to "make" things come into being,

The Power of the "Let There Be"

and you will *take* good with the same ease that you have heretofore taken evil.

You will begin to see what Jesus meant when he "entered in and shut the door," when he went unto his Father state of consciousness and contacted God. Whatsoever he "told" the Father, that was called from the housetops. But he told it in secret. He was not trying to cajole God into doing anything but was finding out just what should be taking place at that moment.

Jesus the personal entered into the impersonal God and lost all his human thought consciousness. In that impersonal blending with God, he was able to see and to let the reality of the kingdom of heaven take place. When he personalized again as Jesus, he always brought the solution of the human problem with him. "The ways of God are past finding out," but they are ways which are greater and stronger than any human thought can imagine. They are ways which are free and not encumbered with the pygmy mind of man—no matter however strong he may appear. "I shall make your enemies your footstool" is the Word. And it is literally so.

So the *let there be* comes into manifestation in the life of the awakened one. He is beginning to see what true prayer is—how he relaxes the conscious mentality, the old wayward thing which was hypnotized with its own importance, and begins to *let* the supernatural become the natural. Presently he finds it easier and easier to *let* ease come into manifestation. It becomes easier to take God than it is to take a cold—which many people claim is very easy.

THE PRISON HOUSE

Human thinking has not only made a madhouse of your body-temple, but also enslaved you, causing you to do its bidding with very little opportunity of escape. From many lifetimes of practice it has gained the whip hand, enforcing its laws ruthlessly and causing your body to do evil when it would have done good, captivating it at will, causing it to commit sickness and sin against every reason or desire.

Until this "strong man" is seen and known for what he is, there is little that can be done about it. It was this very capacity for *free thinking* which caused you to "leave the Garden" so long ago, and since that time, thought has come to be accepted as an actual cause or sub-creator. It is a well-known fact that thinking (mis-thinking is perhaps a better name for it) not only creates its evil pictures which have become so real to you, but also sustains them. Therefore, the moment a thought is broken, the picture being held in place by that thought disintegrates, just as the picture on the screen vanishes the moment the film is cut.

When you begin to understand the truth of "absent from the body and present with the Lord," you will see how the evil in your life can be wiped out. Taking the thought away from evil devitalizes it. How often have you read of some hopeless and helpless invalid having arisen to the full freedom and use of his body during a stress of emotion. It does not matter, for the moment, what caused him to do this impossible thing. It is only interesting that he did it after finding in the best thought that it could not be done. The impossible was done. *The impossible is that which God does all the time as the possible.*

The moment a thing becomes impossible, it is in the realm of the "Father's business" and is entirely beyond the help of thought, although it is a product of thought and is sustained by it. "Be still, and know that I am God" is only one of a thousand admonitions which, if understood, breaks the flow of thought and releases the picture of evil.

The contemplation of God is not in terms of words but a beholding of something which causes breathless adoration. In this state, you perceive the permanent Father-Consciousness to which Jesus continually referred. In other words, behind the shadow of evil thinking stands the perfect creation of God—that which was made in the image and likeness of Him, a little lower than the angels and having dominion over everything, just as the unsullied screen appears the moment the film is snapped. This Father-Consciousness into which you enter at will, by recognition, becomes more and more real, and you see the "strong man" for what he is—a creation of "walking up and down and to and fro" in the realm of illusion.

This mis-thinking has its so-called consciousness, and this is largely a reservoir of evil—a gathering together of the history of evil. Nothing has ever happened to you or your affairs that you did not allow by accepting it. Of course, man protests loudly at this statement. He is sure he did not think of the evil he is experiencing, but if he did not accept it as real for himself, he has accepted it for another. Nothing has happened but that which has been accepted, for it is impossible for anything else to take place.

Once you see the clear connection between body and soul, you will be at the beginning of an ascension which is too wonderful to describe. Not a going up into the air or to the top of the mountain, but an ascension into the real permanent Identity, the Father-Consciousness, wherein all things are possible and from which flows a stream of power which *neutralizes* the oldest problem with ease.

Disabuse your mind that you ascend into any "height," if this means going up. That is all a figure of speech. God is no more on the highest mountain than in the lowest vale. If you can so find it, you have an unbalanced God which destroys all the works of Jesus Christ. Contemplating this All-Presence, you will see that He is just as much present in hell as in heaven and only has to be recognized as there to disintegrate the thought-picture of hell. Likewise, He is just as much in your enemy and most malignant foe as He is in Jesus. But He must be recognized, or else the thinking-pictures of these things will carry on in their evil level of hatred.

Enter into this Consciousness and be glad, for if the child can do it, surely you are beginning to see that you can. Jesus called the people a race of adulterers because they adulterated everything, including the word of God. Only an adult can commit adultery. That is why the kingdom of heaven was given to the child consciousness, for he will not adulterate the power of God to bring out the impossible with his human intellect and findings from his thought-taking basis.

Nothing that Jesus did could have been done through the thought-taking consciousness, for who could reason out any of the so-called miracles? Who can find out how to walk on water, open the eyes of the blind? The moment you start to think about it, it becomes so impossible as to be charged off immediately to hypnotism, magic, miracle, or something supernatural. Yet was it done, and yet were you told to "go thou and do likewise."

It is this glorious revelation of Jesus, showing so clearly the way, that now after these two thousand years is restoring our souls—restoring to us the consciousness of that which was created a little lower than the angels and given dominion over everything.

The Prison House

The pictures of evil created and held in place by thought disappear the moment the thought is taken from them, just as the reflection in the mirror goes nowhere the moment the one standing in front of the glass moves out of range of the mirror. It is so simple and natural.

As you see what Jesus did by "going unto my Father," you begin to awaken from the imprisonment of thought and make some intelligent movement towards your Fatherhood degree. The moment Jesus went unto his Father and became one with Him, he immediately disintegrated all thought-pictures about Him, and when he returned to the personal Jesus again, he brought out the permanency of that consciousness to any who could receive it.

From the personal to the impersonal and back again seems very mystical and will most likely convey some strange, psychic practice. Nothing could be further away from the truth. "Losing your life in order that you shall find it" is another way of putting it.

It is nothing more nor less than an ascending to your Father within. How a thing can come into visibility is beyond all intelligence; the minute it is handled by human thought it just is not there. The mistaken idea that it is something that can be made to appear by affirmations is already proven false. You will either "go in and possess the land," or you will try to create it out of thought, but since the only thing you can create from thought is illusion, a few attempts more at this game of hide and seek with Spirit ought to suffice you.

It doesn't make any difference how it happens. Presently you will become conscious that the temple of God is with man and that every *body* is a temple of the living God, no matter however darkened the temple-body may be to the human thought which is ruling it. The moment the union of body and soul takes place, the cleansing of the temple begins, and the thieves and moneychangers are driven out. It is filled with Light, filled with the consciousness of the Christ, and from this Light flood the rays of real thought.

The reason man is so far from happiness is because he has not yet learned to "be about his Father's business," not knowing that his business is the quintessence of happiness and joy for him. The Father's business, as far as you are concerned, is your business and is what your soul has been seeking to bring to pass, lo these many ages; yet lost in the mist of human thought, you could not see it.

Suddenly you see the wonder of being *still*, and the moment you behold or contemplate this Light, or Father within, at that instant you plunge deep into it and are lost in the Presence. No more thinking or reasoning, but pure *recognition* of the Presence, in which is the fullness of all things. The running to and fro in the thought world ceases, and you can exclaim, "My Lord and my God."

It is wonderful! In this place of the Fatherhood degree of life, you are in the inflow and outflow of the All, and when you come again to the Jesus state, you bring with you the out-picturing of that which you have accepted as real, and it will come through into the flesh.

Through this recognition, gradually will the body be divested of its jailer, and *the strong man shall be bound*. The body will again come into its place of temple, wherein the *light of God* shines through, because the two, body and soul, shall be joined together, never to be separated again, and then the moment you ascend unto the Father you immediately disintegrate all thought-pictures about yourself. Not only do you disintegrate all this maya, or illusion, but you are able to show forth the substance of God.

NONE OF THESE THINGS MOVE ME

The consciousness of "none of these things move me" is a complete blackout for all appearances. It is a sudden elevation above what seems to be, into the place of what actually is. The judging from appearances and the judging righteous judgment are two radically different things. One is judging from what you see with the limited senses, the other recognizing the finished mystery. When Jesus said, "None of these things move me," he refused to enter into an emotional sense of values; hence, he did not recognize the problem first and the ways and means of working it out—he immediately withdrew from the appearances into the place of consummation.

Hell can be transmuted into heaven the moment the "none of these things move me" is true to you. The moment you cease the emotional reaction to appearances, at that moment you have defeated the picture before you, and it will disintegrate.

When you judge from appearances, you are emotionally affected, and this running into the emotional state of life is like leaving the main current of a river and shoving off in a stagnant slough of thought, filled with all sorts of uncleanness. To become emotional about appearances, good or evil, is to get away from the fundamental principle.

You can only become emotional over a thing that appears real to you, and if the appearances are real, then you can do little with them but to side in with them— magnify the evil and thereby bring endless difficulties to pass from the unreal premise. When you leave the clear stream of life for the slough of emotion, you immediately begin making the round of the slough, getting further and further into the muck of human beliefs. You continue in

Without the Smell of Fire

this state until you make the complete circle and again come back to the point from where you departed, or else you succumb and go under by believing the appearances real and true.

Judging the" righteous judgment" is not pronouncing words over a so-called evil situation—it is the judgment of that which *is*. It is turning the attention to the reality of life and not being "moved" by the thing that seems to be. The very sudden *recognition* of this will instantly take out all the fear and evil of the situation and give you a clear solution of what is to be done and accomplished. The moment "it is consummated" takes place in you, the appearances, no matter however terrific, are finished; the last bit of substance has been taken from it, and the old shell will crumple up and disappear.

The emotional handling of a situation inflates it like air does a balloon. Nothing becomes something, until a tiny offense can grow into such proportions that it apparently occupies all space. Does it move you? Then there is something in you which has to come out; there is something in you which can rend you sore, something in you which is going to react emotionally to an appearance and which resents, feels sorry, has pity or sympathy for an appearance of evil and thereby is ready to leave the main current and enter into a slough of beliefs, filled with all sorts of personal uncleanness of thought.

"None of these things move me." Not any of them can change the eternal verities of life. Nothing can change the changeless Principle. Return to this, and the errors of the emotional pattern will disintegrate.

"What is that to thee?" Answer? "What is that to thee?" "Follow thou me," and you will immediately take the inner route to the "it is consummated" state of consciousness. It is either something to you (and if it is, you have your problem to work out), or else it is nothing but an appearance

None of These Things Move Me

and is thereby a passing, changing thing of human thought and emotion.

This divine indifference to the appearances is not a careless handling of the situation. When Jesus was in the consciousness of "none of these things move me," he was still aware that certain mechanics would take place to release the picture from its flames of hell, but he was not moved by the situation. He, being unmoved by the appearances, was able to handle the situation intelligently.

If a savage in the jungle should see an electrical display, he might, judging from appearance, accept all sorts of conclusions. He might be so terrified that he would commit suicide from fear. But the electrician standing by would not be moved by the appearances. Even if it were a very evil manifestation of electricity, he would be able to "judge righteous judgment" and pick up the cause of the evil unemotionally. The moment he did this, the manifestation would cease. The moment you are at the place of "none of these things move me," you can then clearly see what is to be done to disintegrate the picture of evil. It is wonderful!

Remembering that "heaven and earth shall pass away" but not the Word, you have a knowledge of what must happen to all appearances and how transient they all are. All appearances are deceptive, so if you are emotionally moved by them you will build up the structure around them necessary to keep them into manifestation.

RETURNING TO THE ALMIGHTY

If thou return to the Almighty, thou shalt be built up, thou shalt put away iniquity far from thy tabernacles.

Then shalt thou lay up gold as dust, and the gold of Ophir as the stones of the brooks.

Yea, the Almighty shall be thy defense, and thou shalt have plenty of silver.

For then shalt thou have thy delight in the Almighty, and shalt lift up thy face unto God.

Thou shalt make thy prayer unto him, and he shall hear thee, and thou shalt pay thy vows.

Thou shalt also decree a thing, and it shall be established unto thee: and the light shall shine upon thy ways.

When men are cast down, then thou shalt say, There is lifting up, and he shall save the humble person.

He shall deliver the island of the innocent: and it is delivered by the pureness of thine hands.

—Job 22:23-30

"If thou return to the Almighty, thou shalt be built up." There is no question raised as to whether this is possible or not—it simply states that if you return to the Father-Consciousness you will be built up.

Returning from the far country of the illusion, of intelligent matter, to the consciousness of All-power, the Almighty causes this building-up process to take place.

This returning to the Almighty is the return to the "substance of things hoped for, the evidence of things not seen." It can be accomplished only after a full and actual recognition has taken place that you have a father with "enough and to spare." Until this recognition is made, the prodigal sits and wonders if anything is going to happen to change his fearful estate.

At the point of *recognition*, the Prodigal rises and goes in consciousness to the Father. No consideration or thought is taken of the condition the Prodigal is in. He *remembers*—arises and goes. The seeking for the few grains of wheat amidst the husks of relativity is changed to "Then shalt thou lay up gold as dust, and the gold of Ophir as the stones of the brooks."

You cannot do any of this mentally. Thought processes cannot approach it. The nearest it comes to it is through the wise auto-suggestion and the hypnotism of words and affirmations. But all this is "clouds without rain." As long as man tries to think his way out of his difficulties and into the kingdom of heaven, he has reversed the processes of Jesus Christ. Thought radiates from a newly *accepted* state of consciousness, but at no time does it create that state of consciousness. Nothing is changed by thought except the belief of a person.

The most difficult part of all this equation is the complete disregard for all appearances. It is so difficult to keep the attention away from the things and laws and beliefs that swarm in the streets of life. To relax the conscious mentality and let the new way come into being requires a complete turning to the Almighty within and an acceptance that the impossible can and will happen in its own way.

It is impossible for the human thought to imagine that dry land could emerge from wet water. Because it has never happened before is nothing with which to confront the Almighty. There are many things that have never happened before that will happen to you when you "return to the Almighty." There are things that" eye hath not seen, nor ear heard, neither have entered into the heart of man" which are already prepared for those who love the law. There are things to take place entirely outside the law of human thinking. "If ye be in the Spirit, ye are no more under the curse of the law," and you are not trying anymore to measure the results you expect by the limitations of the impossible.

"Come out from among them, and be ye separate." Come out from among them; get away from those demonstrators and talkers of the truth, and you may be able to remember, to arise, to go, and to receive.

You will "speak as one having authority" too, for "when men are cast down, then thou shalt say, there is a lifting up." Do you hear what you will say? It cannot be said from this elevation without something taking place. There is a *lifting up*. Do you hear? "If I be lifted up, I will draw all men unto me."

There is no ambiguity as to what is to be laid up. Gold is called gold and means gold, and the terse reference to the gold of Ophir causes the seeing eye to know that the day of symbolic wealth is over. Too long have metaphysicians said, "I am rich," not realizing that "a rich man cannot enter the kingdom of heaven," and they have only had the symbolic wealth of imagination. It has not been as good as counterfeit money. It is the unborn thing and is worthless in the markets of the world.

But here we have the definite formula for wealth. "If you will return to the Almighty"—no matter where you are, in what condition or how far you have gone afield—if you will recognize this Power and not try to adjust, settle, straighten out anything, but will "turn even unto me with all your heart, ye shall find rest for your soul."

There is a suddenness to recognition. He remembered that his father had enough and to spare—and he arose and went, received and enjoyed, and so will you. Suddenly you will "go in and possess the land," the consciousness of the abundance which you have thus far held in the plane of symbology. Dare you to do this? Dare you to arise within yourself and possess the new consciousness?

"Thou shalt decree a thing, and it shall be established unto thee; and the light shall shine upon thy way."

When you *decree*, you must be at the point of pure recognition, for it is the will of God that is speaking within you. The "God spake" is always followed by "It is done," and the manifestation appears, even as dry land came out of wet water. Do you begin to perceive how the whole course must be altered and changed?

"Think not that I came to destroy." Nothing is to be destroyed; all is to be redeemed, saved and lifted up, and so the heaviness is lifted up and released into joy. Absorption takes place in all of life. The caterpillar is absorbed into the butterfly, the egg into the chicken, Jesus into the Christ, you into your real Christ-Identity, and the fight to destroy anything ceases.

Yes, "if thou return to the Almighty, thou shalt be built up, thou shalt put away iniquity far from thy tabernacles." Iniquity, injustice, inequality—all of these things are only possible to the human consciousness not yet absorbed into the will of God. "When your will is My will and My will is your will, then the will of God is done." And there is no injustice or iniquity in the mind of God. Hence, this absorption is beginning to take place in the awakened consciousness, and it is being made ready to hear the Word. Presently it shall stand at the point of full acceptance of "ye shall decree a thing, and it shall come to pass" because the decreeing shall be done from the point of the will of God.

YET IN MY FLESH

*All flesh shall see it together:
for the mouth of the Lord hath spoken it.*

It does not say all matter, but all *flesh*, for that substance called flesh is a third substance resulting from the merging of matter and Spirit. It is that of which Jesus spoke after his resurrection—the Flesh, real and eternal, changeless, capable of living in the world and yet not of it.

Flesh is impervious to fire and water, can tread upon serpents and scorpions, is not affected by poison, because it is no longer under the curse of the law.

This Flesh is the Jesus Christ Consciousness, the heritage of every man. It is able to move through the pictures of evil without coming nigh destruction. "Ten thousand shall fall at thy right hand ... yet it shall not come nigh thee." Why? Because you have become conscious that you *are* the Jesus Christ Consciousness, the Flesh that is to *see* it. You are so attuned to the Voice that *now*, during these latter days when the cosmic forces are housecleaning the old order of civilization, you can move amid the chaos without fear or evil results.

"The old order changeth" (Tennyson). "Behold, I make all things new." With this great event, the passing of the old order, come many pictures of dissolution and apparent change. It is your time to know whether you can refrain from judging from appearances, or whether you will try to save the old order by looking back. Behold, *I* make all things new—all things—and this making of things new demands that the old pattern be broken up, dissolved and melted down. The fusing of matter and Spirit must take place in order that the kingdom of heaven be established on Earth. You already have this kingdom of heaven in consciousness—now must it create for itself an embodiment by permeating matter and bringing out the Flesh that is to *see* it together.

In this Flesh-consciousness, you are so aligned with the Voice that you can hear It, see the manifestation, touch it, or whatever you will. "This is the way, walk ye in it." You will be able to step over, around, or through the symbolic ladders, scaffolding, mops, buckets, and pans that the great cosmic forces are using to clean up the residue of a broken-down civilization. Behold—the new order!

"Thou shalt keep him in perfect peace, whose mind is stayed on thee." Do you hear? The matter mind cannot be *stayed on Me* (Spirit), because it has not the capacity of this continuity of thought, so filled is it with the history of evil. The Flesh is the substance or medium which receives the new dispensation which is even now descending out of the clouds of belief.

Do you begin to understand this new order? How it is that you are Flesh and that this very recognition causes you to be aware of new urges and concepts which in turn enable you to pass through unharmed? "It shall not come nigh thee." Do you hear?

This Flesh (Consciousness) is a tower of light into which men may run, thereby instantly dissipating all shadows; It is this light, so white and bright that it shines through anything. All darkness and fear are absorbed. All Flesh shall see it together.

You are the tower of Flesh which *sees* the new dimension, or you are the flesh (matter) of which it is said, "Flesh and blood shall not inherit the kingdom of heaven." The Flesh-consciousness which is to see it will also see the things which the matter eyes have not seen, the matter ears have not heard, and find itself possessed of those things which have not entered into the heart of man but which are already prepared for him. It is a new dimension.

Without the Smell of Fire

When you once know yourself as this Jesus Christ Consciousness (Flesh), you will cease the idea of trying to use It as a separate power. A candle does not use light, it gives it, and anything that comes into its radius receives whatever of light it can appropriate. "This is life eternal, to know me." You cannot know Me with the matter mind. All this knowing must be done by the Jesus Christ Consciousness.

This seems so involved, yet it is yours for acceptance, for recognition. The old order of treating, demonstrating, and trying to use God is over. You are God in action when you realize the Jesus Christ *principle of Life*. Anything that touches you then receives the virtue. There is no further effort to heal a disease in the old sense of the word, but a steadfast Light-consciousness that dissolves the congestion of human thought known as disease, poverty, unhappiness, or evil.

It is wonderful! You are It. You are that Christ-Consciousness made manifest in the Flesh. You shall see and shall give all without effort.

All Flesh shall see it together,
for the mouth of the Lord hath spoken it.

TO HIM THAT HATH

To him that hath shall be given ... Now through a glass, darkly, but then face to face.

Recently in a charity drive. a limousine of a famous make was raffled off to raise funds for the refugees. The award went to a man who already possessed seventeen other cars and who greeted the news with, "Good heavens, why didn't someone who wanted and needed a car get it? I have seventeen cars already."

Why did this man, contrary to all the teachings of metaphysics, win the prize? He had no desire for it—didn't want it and was disappointed when it came to him. He held no thought, said no affirmations, declared no truth; in fact, was negative to the whole situation. Why did he win?

Now is the day when the new-old dimension of consciousness is coming into its own. The old worn-out habits of human thinking must give place to the recognition of God. The long years of trying to create a god or trying to use the power of God through thought are over. It is the day of entering into the consciousness of God here and now, a God not created by human thought, neither sustained by it nor made or operated by thought. Consciousness of the Presence has come—it is the second coming of Christ in the individual; the reappearing of the *permanent identity* of man, which automatically lifts him into the place of the finished mystery at which level Jesus expressed.

Jesus always started with the premise "It is done—thank you, Father." He always counseled, "Take no thought," knowing that the thought-taking process would produce only pain.

The more you hear a person making affirmations the more you know he is not, and has not, the thing he affirms.

Without the Smell of Fire

A rich man never affirms that he is rich, because he *is* rich; a well man never affirms he is well, because he *is* well, and so Jesus started with the premise "It is done—it is consummated." Entering this consciousness, he functions from that level and automatically produces the manifestations of that consciousness, just as a writer produces books and a singer songs. There is nothing strange about it. The God-created being who recognizes himself will produce the things of Spirit.

All this is beyond the grasp of human thinking. It is in the realm of the impossible and therefore must come under the law of God, where all things are possible. Until man sees this, he will perpetually try to "work" the law of God and attempt to make God do his bidding.

The acquisitive quality that automatically sets in the moment you enter the new Consciousness is as natural as its opposite in the mental realm. There is nothing that can stop the flow of manifestation. It is as automatic as the casting of a reflection in a mirror. You do nothing, but you are perfectly conscious of yourself as a body, and therefore the reflection of it takes place whenever you pass before the reflector, or the mirror. There is nothing strange about this, and so the moment you enter your Father-Consciousness, you begin to release automatically the perfect reflection of that state of consciousness. To the consciousness of substance, you automatically express substance in the relative world—you do not demonstrate anything. Thus Jesus, with his eternal question: "Believest thou?"

Can you by any chance appropriate this consciousness? The moment you do, the whole universe becomes new. You exclaim, "Whereas before, I was blind, now I can see," that is, you have entered into a consciousness of sight, and you automatically see.

Hence, all the positive thinking in the world is not going to make anything happen, just as all the negative thinking in the world is not going to change God. It may change your outlook on life and your belief, but thought will never change anything in the perfect universe of God.

The man who won the car didn't need it, didn't want it. Hundreds of others did, and perhaps many of them "knew they were going to get it." But it went automatically to the one with the consciousness which could accept it without the excitement of having made a demonstration.

Entering this consciousness is no more difficult for you than anyone else if you but once glimpse the fact that it is something beyond thought and reason. No reasoning can be used on Spirit any more than it can be applied to Santa Claus. The fact that the child can believe is sufficient to make the Santa appear. The moment you *believe*, the body for your new acceptance begins to appear. This is all too fantastic to be true—and of course, it is not true to the level of thought in which you dwell. Nothing can happen through that level but more thought-pictures of evil.

The moment the new idea is accepted, the announcement of the coming into being of the new idea goes forth—the shepherds see the light of the star and move towards the place of birth with their gifts. In other words, the moment you can *believe*, you have announced to the world that a new idea is to be brought forth, and *everything* that is to assist in the coming into being of this new idea responds and moves toward the place of manifestation. It is too fantastic to think about, but the moment you enter into a new consciousness, everything that is necessary to bring that consciousness into being moves toward you—the wise men bearing gifts or recognition. Through all this apparent mysticism, you begin to see how it is that your new consciousness is embodied and made real.

Your body is the body of God. All living manifestation is the body of God, the place where the invisible comes through into expression. Without a body, there would be no God visible. Without an automobile, the principle of locomotion in that respect would be invisible, nothing, yet would it be there always. Your body is the body of God. Do you hear? Does that by any chance mean anything to you? Contemplate this: "Be still, and know that I am God" and see if anything filters through into your relative place of thought. Gradually you will not only understand why you are not sick anymore but also why it is impossible for that to happen. You will again approximate the consciousness of being created in the image and likeness of God and see how this slight adjustment through "believe" causes you to be every whit whole.

The evil thought-pictures that have covered your body disappear the moment you recognize that your body is the body of God. You can carry this wonderful idea into a further place—that the body of God is a fit place for God to dwell and that the Father within you has an express service and manifestation into the world. No wonder Jesus dismissed everything in favor of "wist ye not that I must be about my Father's business?" It is amazing how this recognition suddenly aligns you with the proper expression in life. You are every whit whole. You are the body of God, and the Lord in the midst of you is strong and mighty.

Your prayer is: "The Lord is in his holy temple, let all the earth rejoice." Your whole body and manifestation is rejoicing because now you know that your body is the body of God, and the Lord in His holy temple is filling you full of the joy of living.

The announcement of your Self causes everything that has to do with that Self to awaken and come to the place of recognition. That which you affirm from the consciousness of "it is done" is confirmed by the world. The fame of this new announcement goes out in all directions.

FOLLOW ME

Made in the image and likeness of the I AM, perfect and eternally sustained by the unchanging power of the Presence; dwelling eternally in a state of paradise, functioning in harmony and above all the laws of the human mind. This is spiritual man born equal one with the other.

"Conceived in sin, born in iniquity, his days few and full of trouble," his actions such that when he would do good, he does evil; his heritage an accumulation of beliefs from his family, his environment, and even his past lives. Fighting always against hopeless odds—eternally warring against sin, sickness, and death.

This is the mortal creation, the sub- or mis-creation, a product of thought. As he thinketh, so is he, yet he cannot stop the flow of thought he has set in action, which is keeping his John Smith in an eternal stream of evil. He learns and earns by the sweat of his brow. A hopeless situation at the outset—he must wait and wait and wait for everything to happen. He rails against his destiny at the very moment he is setting more of the evil into operation. Thought is the source and sustenance of all this evil and the impetus of it.

"Arise, walk through the land in the length of it and in the breadth of it, for I will give it unto thee." Arise, walk through the land in the length of it and in the breadth of it, for I will give it unto thee, A repetition of this wonder is in order, for no matter where it finds you, it is for you. Though one hundred and twenty years old, "his eye was not dim, nor his natural forces abated."

We are moving through the time of human thought (a thousand years may be as a day) to the permanent events of spiritual existence. In other words, everything has already happened in the perfect creation. Our getting to it is through the beliefs of human thought, very much like looking through the wrong end of a telescope—we see that which is really close at hand, miles away. The moment we actually *see*, we find it at hand. It is the "look again" of Spirit, which does not need the four months of human hypnotism and belief to make so, but only the adjusting of vision. Jesus could make this appear because he was so conscious of it. He could see through the human time-space of thought and perceive the perfect, completed kingdom of heaven here and now.

Into whatsoever level of human consciousness you enter, that becomes the *absolute* truth to you, and you become hypnotized to that level of thought. You are then under the direct power of the race consciousness of the said level of thought. The stronger the belief the more reality *you* give it.

Hence, we find people who apparently are of normal intelligence entering into all sorts of cults and beliefs, and getting a measure of results from them. The good results are small, but the evil is enormous, for every one of them is motivated by the worship of gold and personality. All of the tenets of the cult become laws so absolute that to break them is far greater than the breaking of the laws of God. Cursing and damning and all sorts of black magic ensue to the follower who dares leave the fold. And while the same student can see a thousand and one places where the power of the cult has ignominiously failed to do the least thing, when it comes to cursing and damning and personal injury he will quake with fear at the supposed power, not realizing he is giving it all the power it ever had by believing in it. Once he breaks this connection, he finds it nothing and sees it from a new level of consciousness.

Watch. Let no man deceive you. Follow no man—follow Me. If you follow no man, no man can deceive you. Do you hear? Follow Me.

ASCENSION

So much talk about ascension. It has come to mean a going up of the physical body instead of entering into another degree of consciousness. "If I be lifted up (to a new state of consciousness), I will draw all men (manifestation) unto me." That is, I will appropriate and experience everything that is in that consciousness. But that apparent being lifted up does not indicate anything physical. When Jesus ascended unto his Father-Consciousness, he did not go anywhere physically. He entered into a fourth-dimensional consciousness wherein the things that were formerly true were no longer true. The consciousness of the Fatherhood degree does not find itself a sort of Overlord, looking down upon the Son.

It is amazing that the simplicity of Jesus' teaching could have been so distorted as to indicate that the body would have to go anywhere in order to ascend. The moment you ascend to your Father, you find the new level of things, real, natural, and simple, whereas before, it was all unreal. What is true in the three-dimensional consciousness is wholly untrue in the Fatherhood degree.

"I go unto my Father (hood)" consciousness, and there I am no longer under the curse of the law—yet am I under the law. Coming into the consciousness of your Fatherhood does not indicate that you do not obey the law. You still render unto Caesar the things which are Caesar's and unto God the things which are God's, but you are not caught in the curse of it all. It is wonderful!

For some reason or other, man has accepted the ascension as something so mystical and so impossible that it is clothed in the magic of a fairy tale. It is supposed to be accompanied by the embodiment of an unearthly looking individual wearing fluttery robes of a color and texture to suit the person ascending—a sort of theatrical finale. Yet nothing could be further away from the truth, as testified by Jesus when he asked his disciples to come and place their hands in his side and in his palms and see that "a spirit" (what most people believe to be the next state) "has not flesh and blood." So it is a happy revelation to you that you are going to ascend into the *Flesh body* (used as we understand it in the quotation "yet in my flesh shall I see God" to mean the fusion of body and soul).

You are ascending all the time. As a balloon from which ballast is thrown enters different strata of atmosphere, so do you go into a new level of consciousness and therein appropriate, as natural and normal, those things which you find, just as a body entering a warm room takes on the temperature of the room.

Much is said of the Second Coming. Few recognize that it is taking place right at this moment. Not the second coming of Jesus, for he has never gone away. Our vision is so dense that it cannot sustain his brightness on our level of consciousness—that is all. The second coming of Christ, the Fatherhood degree, is actually taking place at this moment, just as the millennium is also taking place and is entering now into the picture. It is the unseen leaven that is leavening the whole mass of meal, unconsciously and unseen, for that is the way the second coming is to be, through the clouds of your belief and as a thief in the night.

This coming is actually taking place at this moment. The government is to be upon His shoulders. That too is coming and, in spite of opinions and beliefs, the cosmic power is hurrying along the word of Jesus: "*This* is the kingdom of heaven"—*this*, right here, the now. The second coming is actually taking place in the temples of men. When you see Jesus again, he will not say, "My kingdom is not of this world," for that world is passing away. It is being disintegrated and re-established as the kingdom of heaven.

The old subconscious mind is being stirred up, and its old habits and beliefs are being put through such a *light* treatment as to disabuse them of any power whatsoever. You, of course, have to make yourself as God. That is the way you were created—in the image and likeness, a little lower than the angels, given dominion over everything over and under. So you can begin to see why you must, as Jesus did, make yourself as God—appropriate your divinity and begin to see the dominion you have over all the foul beliefs that have separated your body and soul. You have wandered into a far land, and it has been full of false things from which you have drawn your conclusions. But at last you are awakening and beginning to see. It is wonderful!

In the Fatherhood degree (which is your permanent Identity, changeless and eternal), you find the finished mystery; you find the fulfilled desire. It is the state of consciousness into which Jesus ascended when he said, "Thank you, Father; I knew that this was already done, but these ... so I said thank you." Do you begin to see that Jesus was not working out problems but revealing the new dimension?

Furthermore, do you begin to see what entering into this Fatherhood degree means to you? It means that you escape the curse of the law. Not the Law but the curse of the law. So all the pseudo laws that function evilly over man are made null and void in this consciousness. The laws of any of the quasi-sciences, with their dark and terrible fate of evil, are all neutralized. All the old terrible fate pictures turn out to be clouds without rain—in other words, you discover you are no more under the curse of the law of human fate. Human fate is what Jesus came to destroy or set aside. And this he did by ascending to the

Fatherhood degree of consciousness, which was not concerned with the man-made laws.

Again, the second coming of Christ must not be confused with Jesus. Your body, called what you will, is the temple of the living God, but until the union of body and soul is made, the body cannot receive any of the inspiration of the soul. It cannot "step down" its desires or give them a body, because there is a gulf of belief that has separated matter and Spirit. They are two substances foreign to each other, the one wholly intelligent and powerful, the other filled with all sorts of beliefs in separation. But once this union is made and you know that the body is the temple of the living God, you soon will see the law "you must decrease, I must increase" taking place. The former belief and power of the body separated from Soul are taken away, and it becomes merely the temple through which the Light comes into manifestation. When this begins to happen, the limitations of John Smith are dissipated. "Whereas before, I (as John Smith) was blind, now I can see." Just like that—just entering into the consciousness of "it is done," and if it is done, it is quite natural and simple of expression.

When you begin to make your *ascension* into the consciousness of the permanent Identity (the claiming or assumption of your heritage), you will begin also to experience many wonderful things, too numerous to mention, like the sands of the sea. In the way "ye know not of" do they come into being. They are embodied, for now you know that is the purpose of your new temple and that the second coming gives you the *authority* which you as John Smith lacked.

"Marvel not, ye must be born again." There is no question about it. This ascension, or being born again, is not a strange psychic thing, but the most beautiful experience in the world, an awakening to that which eternally *is*. It is so filled with light and gladness that you again experience the joy of life. "I came that your joy might be full."

As man begins to understand the difference between *thought* and *consciousness*, he will also experience the ascension quite naturally. Thought is the creator and the sustainer of all evil manifestation, which in turn is maya, illusion. The fact that you consider sickness curable from a human standpoint proves its very unreality. The moment thought is taken away from a manifestation, that manifestation disintegrates and falls to pieces. "Be absent from the body and present with the Lord" bespeaks the wisdom of the Lord. Real thought does not create consciousness, but emanates from a state of consciousness, and the mis-thought and misconception is merely a counterfeit of the emanation of Light-thought which the Christ-Consciousness exudes.

It is easy to understand why Jesus counseled, "Take no thought," and asked, "Who by taking thought ...?" We are beginning to understand the difference between thought and consciousness. Consciousness is a *permanent* thing. The moment you ascend to any level of consciousness, an entirely new set of thoughts emanates from that point, as rays of light emanate from the sun. The mis-creation of human thinking which has been walking "up and down and to and fro" in the world of appearances is real only to the believer in it, and its manifestations of evil must be fed and sustained by thought.

The moment you *ascend* to any level of consciousness, you have the strength and power of all consciousness at that level—just as the moment you descend to any level of human thinking you have the entire race consciousness on that level to aid, abet, and prove the truth of the evil manifestation. Hence, if you have a given disease in your thought creation, every bit of evil knowledge, together with every proof of that disease, helps, aids, and abets your thought in making it real and fixed in your world. You have the entire race consciousness of the evil you are holding onto by thought to back up your arguments that it is real and eternal. No mistake about this—you have the undivided support of everything on the level of consciousness to which you ascend.

WITH ALL THY GETTING

The great difference between Jesus Christ and his followers is that he *became* the power by being conscious of it instead of using it or trying to make it operate in a lesser dimension. This difference, which may appear on the surface to be merely a play on words, when once examined shows such a gulf between the two approaches as to make that separation between Dives and Lazarus seem nothing but a crevice.

Being conscious of a power causes the manifestation of that power to be natural, orderly, and at the command of the person in such a place. Nothing strange takes place when a switch is turned and a room is filled with light, music, warmth, cool air, color, and now even odors. It is a natural following of the proper understanding of electricity. Franklin recognized something of this when he sent up his kite with a key tied to its tail, but the freak happenings of lightning as compared to the intelligent employment of electricity are likened unto the so-called miracles, supernatural happenings, as compared to the revelation of Jesus Christ.

The moment a statement like that is made, the old human intellect immediately raises its hydra head into the limelight and says, "Such things are too deep for the average man." In the instruction book, it says that "a child can do it" but an adult cannot, because he wants to adulterate it with personal opinions and beliefs, hearsay and findings of human power. Nevertheless, Jesus was right when he prefaced this glorious revelation with the words "a child can do it."

A child can do it because a child will not try to put the fourth dimension through the "glass, darkly" of human reasoning. Remembering that "the wisdom of man is foolishness in the eyes of God," there is no use to put the God-wisdom through the human miasma of beliefs if you expect to get anything but a distorted picture of evil.

When Jesus was confronted by a picture of evil, he immediately retired into the consciousness of the Christ within, the Father within, and became one with Him. This Father within, he said, was within every man, awaiting recognition. It was not a power to be used, but a power to *become*—a blending with the true Self, the Christ-mind.

He took his human consciousness, as it were, into the inner, and when he returned, it was purified of the belief in a power opposed to God. Very much the same as a child might take a bucket of dirty water to the ocean, throw it in, and return with the same bucket filled with pure water. So when Jesus came again from the Father-Consciousness, the situation was entirely clarified. The personal became the impersonal—that is, it was lost in the Father-Consciousness, which is "of too pure eyes to behold iniquity," and when he personalized again, he brought forth what to the human sense was healing, or revelation, but which was just as natural to the Consciousness within as the appearance of light in a house wired for light. It was and is a natural thing.

Many people believe that God is sitting on high, waiting to pounce on them for doing what they apparently cannot help doing. No wonder the constant "awake thou that sleepest, and Christ shall give thee light."

The unnaturalness of Truth must be wiped out by the understanding given to us by Jesus Christ. Discovering this permanent, changeless identity within himself and every man, he was amazed that no one seemed to understand the simplicity of stepping into the Father-Consciousness and thereby neutralizing the appearances of evil in the Jesus body.

Without the Smell of Fire

A thousand and one things have been approximated by the understanding of electricity. Time and space have practically been eliminated by its use. To hear a man speaking thousands of miles away is nothing, and to transmit photographs through the air along with voices and other things is everyday fare now. So will the power of God one day become as natural and normal because you will move into the consciousness of its reality and stop imagining that something mysterious and wonderful is to happen which is to upset your life with the thing called "miracle." When you arrive at the simple understanding of Jesus Christ, you will find the supernatural natural. When you enter into this consciousness of Life, you will find sickness quite unnatural and quite impossible.

This is the state of consciousness Jesus discovered in every man, and it was this permanent Father-Consciousness in the man to which he addressed his questions: "Believest thou this? Will you receive your sight? Will you be made whole?" It was not to the confused human thought which found itself in a maze of evil and impossible situations. In spite of the statements apparently to the contrary, Jesus did not come to heal people nor yet to help them, if this is taken to mean some temporary relief. He came to reveal the Fatherhood dimension of Life, which was able and capable of bringing forth what the human mind called miracles, with a naturalness and ease which it found in Itself.

The difference in demonstrating power and being conscious of it is vast. A lion goes to the water hole when he will; he does not have to wait for the most auspicious moment. He does not have to consider anything. He is unafraid of the other animals. Yet he does not try to generate this power of courage. He does not have to make a demonstration; he does not have to use the power. He is just unafraid because he is conscious of his power. He does not use power—he *is* power. While this illustration is quite inadequate to cover the idea, yet will it give some inkling of what Jesus discovered within every man: a superb power, or the Presence, which enabled him to *be* and *let* instead of using or trying to make a demonstration of it.

There is nothing against the demonstration, but revelation of your Christ-Consciousness enables you to see a different basis of operation. As soon as you see this even faintly, you will begin to understand the power in such words as *let there be*. This is not demonstration but is merely releasing the manifestation into visibility—releasing the invisible or stepping down the power into manifestation. You continue with this until you start to reason and find out that it is impossible.

The moment you start to reason about how God can do it and why He doesn't, you might just as well stop, for you are approaching something which is impossible to the human thought. "No man knows." "The ways of God are past finding out."

The moment man sees he has a permanent Identity eternally knocking at the door of his human consciousness asking to come into expression, he will open unto Him and let Him in. The Jesus and Christ become one consciousness called "Jesus Christ," the Word made flesh and the flesh made Spirit, and this is the unbeatable combination of Flesh—the Flesh which "shall see it together," and the "yet in my flesh."

Through the Bible, you see the commands addressed to the "hearing ear" and the "seeing eye," the command which is misunderstood by the three-dimensional human thought consciousness.

"The cattle on a thousand hills are mine ... if I were hungry, I would not tell thee." I would "slay and eat."

What to do with such a statement? One cannot demonstrate it, no matter how hard he tries. The cattle on a thousand hills are only his when he can accept them, and he cannot enter in and kill and eat with impunity unless he is in that consciousness. This is done not in the pompous conceit of the human mind, but in the utter humility of recognition. Through this contact, he is able to step the invisible down into manifestation. In other words, whatsoever he can and does tell this Father within, that is he able to bring forth into manifestation as a natural revelation instead of a demonstration. He finds it natural to "go in and possess the land" because he is conscious of it. He is able to appropriate his own not by argument but by revelation. Jesus saw this so clearly he could even say, "Thank you, Father" before the manifestation had taken place.

"You sought me for the loaves and fishes and did not see the miracle" explains the surprise of Jesus. He had shown the ways and means of the manifestation, yet the crowd of followers still sought him for the manifestation. Things, demonstrations, manifestations, and signs—all that is what the unenlightened mind seeks because it still believes in a God apart from man. When the Word "signs shall follow, they do not precede" is heard, then will you be able to "watch with me one hour."

The most important hour in the life of Jesus was that one hour, and there were the disciples all asleep—probably snoring, getting ready for the big Roman holiday—going back into their former beliefs. "What, could you not watch with me one hour?" Could you not stand and see the *miracle* instead of looking for the manifestation?

So is it with consciousness versus thinking and demonstrating. When you *believe* and stand on that point, the signs will follow; you will know that they will follow, and all the excitement of demonstration will have passed. "Lightning never strikes twice in the same place," and so is it with demonstrations. One big demonstration is about all any student or follower of the truth ever gets. He keeps on living from the light of that one thing instead of entering into the place of Power where that thing is natural. He continues to expect lightning to strike again in the same place.

Do you begin to see that the sign has already been given and now you are to enter into the "miracle" of the thing instead of waiting for further manifestations? Do you begin to understand how it is that in the Father-Consciousness you shall "go in and possess the land" without the silly idea that you have done something strange? When the "virtue" proceeded out of Jesus, do you suppose he forced it out or made it go out of him? Or do you think it just had to go out automatically because he had been touched? Answer for yourself, and you will begin to understand the difference between mental and spiritual revelation. The virtue went out because it is the nature of God to answer any and all prayers automatically the moment He is touched by recognition and acceptance.

"Solitude reveals all its secrets to the one who is alone with God, and wraps him in all its charm."

"Come out from among them" and be free—enter into your Consciousness.

"Then the solitude taught him to draw on the treasury of reverie."

"Enter in and be saved." Enter into what? Enter into this consciousness of the Presence, this permanent Identity to which Jesus constantly referred. When you "enter" you do not push, shove, beat, fight, nor are you dragged in—you enter. It is the same power wrapped in the word that makes it possible. When you begin to see the *power* of the Word, you will see why My words are power and they are Spirit, and they "shall not return unto me void, but shall accomplish whereunto they are sent." It is wonderful when you are en rapport with the Spirit of the Word.

Without the Smell of Fire

When a thing is accepted in the consciousness, the body (Jesus) is able to materialize it. When you have accepted the fact that you can write a letter, the body can make it become flesh, as it were. So with all prayer. When you "ask, believing that you receive," it is so—but it is not to be a demonstration. I may watch and memorize some chords or notes on a piano and be able to play them, as long as I remember them and make a certain kind of music, but never can I say I am a musician. So is it with the Christ-Consciousness.

Enter in and be saved. Go in and possess all the land. It is wonderful!

CONSCIOUSNESS

From Consciousness flows a never-ending stream of light, which in turn manifests itself in all sorts of by-products. Take, for example, the consciousness that the world at large has of Lincoln, and then try to list or catalog the books, plays, articles, anecdotes, and sayings which have flown therefrom, to say nothing of the statues, paintings, and the millions of souvenirs.

This illustration, while inadequate to express the idea that Jesus conveyed by going to the Father, or Consciousness, in a way gives some idea of what happens to the individual when he perceives the consciousness of a thing. The consciousness is a reality, and the moment it is approximated, the manifestation begins to flow. All thought proceeds from consciousness and does not in any way contribute to it or take from it.

You cannot create real consciousness by taking thought; you only create a false thing. Imagine trying to create a Lincoln by thought. He would be a character in fiction, without reality and without embodiment, a temporary thing at best. Yet man continues to try to create a consciousness of health, prosperity, or happiness by taking thought, in spite of the warning of Jesus: "who by taking thought?"

The established consciousness, the finished thing, when entered into yields manifestation, whether this be of health, prosperity, or happiness. The thought-created pseudo-consciousness of any of these things yields nothing. "Clouds without rain" is the measure of the state of things created by thought. There is no life in any manifestation concocted by thought, no matter what it is. Willpower sometimes accomplishes a semblance of power, but its day is short.

Trying to bring a little warmth out of a room is more or less a failure, though you might bring a warmed blanket from it, which would in a measure bring something of that consciousness down to the present condition. But its duration is short, and presently you must go again for another warm blanket.

So is it with all things. "Eye hath not seen, nor ear heard, neither have entered into the heart of man the things that are prepared." Understand that the things you are seeking are prepared and waiting for you to enter into the consciousness of this truth. The moment you come to the consciousness that they are already prepared, you have made an enormous stride forward into the place of realization. Just think what it means to you to suddenly discover that the things you have been seeking to demonstrate actually exist, are real and ready to be brought into manifestation. Half of the battle with thought is over.

Accepting this mentally with the hope that you can demonstrate it is a fallacy. Anything you *try* to do fails. You cannot "mock God." Whatsoever you have in your mind, that will be your exact result. So do not think to trick this God-power by believing in a new formula.

The fact that you finally discover that the place is actually prepared and waiting does not make it appear. It then has to be appropriated, and you cannot appropriate it unless it is natural and normal. Any anxiety, excitement, or curiosity as to whether it will work or not forms an impassable barrier.

Jesus did not try to work any miracles on the Jesus plane of consciousness. He immediately ascended to the Fatherhood degree, where the thing that Jesus sought was an established fact. Acknowledging this (telling his Father in secret), he was then able to bring this wonderful thing out through the Jesus body. It all seems involved but it is natural and easy. It is so simple that a child can perform it, for the child can accept without reservations and without the human element of trying to prove things. An open acknowledgment that God knows more than any man you ever knew might help. And if you should be able to take this stance, then you should, in order to follow up your discovery, ask of God instead of a man.

Behold, *I* am He that should come. The permanent Identity, the Father within you, is He that should come, and you will presently stop looking for another.

Do not get the idea of Jesus confused in your mind. Jesus could do nothing of himself—neither can you, and that gives you an equal start. Having been assured that you have the Father-Consciousness within, the same mind that was also in Christ Jesus, you will understand how very wonderful your situation is. You are placed in a position to perform the works done by Jesus Christ because you have the authority and the ability and the knowledge of how they were done.

The moment you see this, you will discount not only what every man has told you regarding yourself and the conditions of the world, but what you have been telling yourself, and presently the old history of your John Smith will fall away. It will be so completely transcended that it will not come into mind anymore.

You see the Jesus passing back and forth from the Father to the Son consciousness. You see him going unto the Father (his perfect Identity) and there acknowledging that which he wished to appear, from the personal to the impersonal and back again, bringing with it the substance in manifestation. It is wonderful! And so it is.

The prepared place, the thing prepared, the blessings that you cannot receive because they are so immeasurably greater than your little human mind with its greed has been able to take in—all this awaits recognition. You cannot recognize it until you have gotten over the idea of bringing

God down into manifestation, or healing. Nothing is more absurd than a testimony that God healed one part of the body while another remained ill. This is too ridiculous to mention. The Presence does not work that way. The consciousness of the Presence when contacted makes you every whit whole.

You will notice that Jesus always went to his Father-Consciousness. He never tried to bring It down to the level of the John Smith thinking. If he could have done this, it would have acted from that level. But he went unto his Fatherhood-Consciousness and there found the finished thing, which he was able then to release through the temple—Jesus. It is all so simple that it is given to the child, yet so difficult to the adulterous adult.

"I go to prepare a place for you," and I take my body with me. We see the insistence of Jesus: "Yet in my flesh shall I see God." Jesus was the only teacher who materialized; he was the only way-shower who brought forth the invisible and discovered that everything that was to come to him must be "stepped down" through his temple, body, which had been merged with the Spirit. The Father and Son become one, making a perfect medium for the God-power to rush through into manifestation.

All this seems vague in words, yet if you are at the point of recognizing what Jesus said to you two thousand years ago, you will at last see that "whatsoever you ask in my nature, that give I unto you" is more than a statement. It is the actual manifestation. Whatsoever you can accept as finished and done is capable of coming into manifestation in the body.

Matter merged with the Spirit—the body and soul joined together—brings man back to his primal beauty and power. He is again conscious of his true Self and able to bring forth the manifestations as shown by Jesus. Yes, and even greater things than these will ye do. It is wonderful when you know you do not have to bring God down to your level of thinking, but that you move into the Consciousness and therein function from the level of what you recognize as possible. No matter about the mechanics—they will take care of themselves. They will be handled easily and naturally.

If the desire or urge is given to you, you can fulfill it if you recognize the permanent Identity, the Being which was created perfect and remains eternally so, the Fatherhood degree, the point where contact is definitely and effectively made with God. It is wonderful!

A spider goes within for the substance with which to spin his web. Presently you will believe Jesus Christ and go within your consciousness and find all that you have been looking for on the outside or that you have been trying to create.

THE ANSWERED PRAYER

According to Jesus Christ, every prayer is answered before it is asked. "Before you ask, I will answer, and while you are yet speaking, I will give it unto thee."

Either you have come to a place where you believe this as a factual thing, or else you are still toying with the mysterious thing called prayer, which is merely wishing or hoping that some strange thing will come into action which will change things. But if the prayer is answered before the asking and this is once known to you—not thought of but *known* as an actual reality—then will you be headed at last in the right direction for manifestation, for precipitation, for the walking on the water, levitation, and a thousand and one other things that your former "praying" (beseeching) consciousness hoped to attain.

Once you grasp this truth even in a small way, you will release all the longing and the wishing. Your prayer then will become a definite *speaking of the word*, backed up by the "it is done consciousness."

For ages man has prayed for the kingdom to come on earth, yet it has been here always, awaiting recognition. It seems incredible when viewed from the revelation of Jesus Christ.

The *stepping-down* into visibility of the invisible heaven which is already here is a matter of personal recognition. If you cannot believe that it is so—that it is done—it cannot take form or shape, because it needs this *recognition* to bring it into visibility. Strange as it may seem, you are the only one who can perform this peculiarly interesting action. It is your recognition of the "it is done" state of things that enables you to give it a body and form.

The Answered Prayer

Do you begin to understand the command "Be still, and know that I am God"? Have you ever been *still*? Have you ever been able to stop the whole racket of trying to get things and been able to contemplate the deep, mysterious thing called "it is done"? It is not a thing that can be talked over with another. It is something, an *elevation of consciousness*, at which you have arrived through the light emanating from pure recognition of truth; something which transcends thought and is at a level of beholding.

The moment this *it is done* state of things takes place within you, the anxiety, the curiosity, the fear all depart, and a divine *abandon* overtakes you. You relax into peace; yea, a "peace which passeth all understanding." The ways and means of the appearing are entirely outside any human thought process. There is nothing that can be done from the outside that will in any way aid or assist the coming into manifestation of this consciousness.

"Come out from among them and be ye separate." Suddenly you are beginning to understand the finished thing, called heaven on Earth, for which you have been praying so long and for which the nations of the world are clamoring. It is wonderful; the thing you have been seeking has been edging towards you for expression, and you would not. You turned from the real to the shadow. You kept looking for a body and form and not for the soul of the miracle, looking for the loaves and fishes and not for the power which brought them into being. Once you see the Power and recognize It, the embodiment will take care of itself. The moment this "it is done" comes to be a reality to you, you will *see*, for the eye becomes single and recognizes that which *is* instead of the disintegrating forms of matter.

Hence, we see Jesus with the hungry multitude, obliterating every human law. What matter though the agriculturist for a thousand years had said it takes four months to

Without the Smell of Fire

raise wheat, and it must be harvested and milled, etc.? No matter, for the answered prayer comes through whenever it is recognized as "it is done," no matter what happens in the relative world.

The very one who stands with such force against the Principle will suddenly turn about and render a decision that is entirely in agreement with the words. The thief will suddenly give; something will cause him to act in a manner which he never knew before, and against his personal ideas. He may rail against it all after it is over, and run to and fro in the desert trying to find the man *making the bread*—who is not there any longer.

"When ye pray, believe that ye receive, and it shall be so." *Receive* in the present tense. If you cannot believe, accept, recognize that you receive at the moment of prayer, you will not be able to step it down, for the anxiety, wonder, and excitement will keep it from manifestation.

To the thought-taking person, all this is just words—and that is all it is. He is still desirous of seeing it work or wants to talk it over with someone.

When you begin even faintly to recognize "it is done," then you will see that the bringing of your prayer into materialization is a matter of aligning your temple-body with the Christ.

This morning when I awakened, this article came through to me. It was already done—I accepted it and *let* it come through into visibility. That is why you are reading it now. Had I first discussed it with others, the inspiration would have gone out of it, just as all the life will go out of champagne when it is uncorked. If you want results in this new day, you will have to be silent about the *inner* plane revelation.

First you must find out whether you actually *believe* or whether you would "like to believe." Whether you are seeking Me for the loaves and fishes, or whether you are seeking Me for the glory of the Power. You can profess anything you like with your lips, but what about your heart? What do you profess with your heart? What do you feel?

If you want Me because of *things*, then you will get nothing, for the very greediness for things shows plainly that you do not believe the law of heaven on Earth. It shows that you are still believing in the teaching of Jesus Christ as a wonder-working power that will give you things you could not otherwise have. You will fail—your temple-consciousness is filled with thieves and dove sellers, all of which must go before you can make it a fit dwelling place for the Light.

When the greediness is not there, it is because you recognize the inalienable right you have to the kingdom of heaven. The kingdom of heaven is not some imaginary thing you must demonstrate in order to show you have power. The kingdom of heaven is a state of consciousness from which all things come into manifestation. It is wonderful. And it is here and now if you can grasp the revelation of Jesus Christ. A child can—can you? Or is the anxiety so keen within you that it veils the lovely heaven here and now and causes you to wander for years in a wilderness of human thought, systems, organizations, people? Eventually you will dispense with all this and return to Me and have peace.

Lately thousands of people who for years have followed the best approved systems and organizations of truth have found it does not work and have gone back to their pills and beliefs. It is no uncommon thing to hear someone say, "Well, I was in this, that, or the other for twenty, thirty, forty years, and now I know that it was all imagination." They are sincere, but never once in the long journey through personalities and organizations did they believe "it is done." They said it, but they did not believe it, and it is plainly stated that "when ye pray, believe that you receive, and it shall be so." *Believe*—present tense. It has to be accepted as a natural, normal thing, and it shall be so. How, why, when, where is entirely out of your hands.

There is no more light coming out of the dark, ancient teachings from foreign lands. All the hypnotic, strange voodoo practices that issue forth under grand and glorious names are only more snares. If you think any man has a trick up his sleeve that is going to help you on your spiritual unfoldment, it is because you do not believe in Jesus Christ, and as long as you do not believe in Jesus Christ you cannot "get into the sheepfold." There is no chance for you to enter into the place of realization. You can be so attracted by a robe and a turban or a fine house with the cast-off luxuries of the former rich that you mistake this for Me. It is true *I* move amid luxuries, through poverty and through all the thought forms, for they are nothing but just that. The moment the Me is recognized, then they, the thought forms, disintegrate and are blown away by the breath of Spirit.

"When you pray"—what do you do? Is your attitude that of a naughty child receiving forgiveness? "Behold, I make all things new." This is the cloud of illumination which has suddenly descended upon you, and the "it is done" is seen, heard, felt, touched, and tasted in this glorious Light. It is so completely done and comprehended that you come from prayer in a state of continual *peace* which passeth all understanding—all, yea, *all* the understanding of the beliefs through which you have been passing.

No matter of what duration the belief may have been when the prayer was made, then comes the enlightenment, the freedom, the stepping-up into the Fatherhood degree which immediately steps down the manifestation.

This prayer is such that it enables you to "look again" and see for yourself. You are entering the "alone path," the place where you move into expression through *recognition*. It is wonderful! "Look again." What kind of prayer is that? That was the kind Jesus Christ said—pure, unadulterated recognition of the "it is done," which, remember, entirely nullifies all human law, no matter however time-honored.

Most of all must you recognize the *ease* with which Jesus prayed. There is no hard work about it at all. There is no straining to be spiritual, no changing the voice to what is known as a deep reverent tone, for there is nothing in all this but emotionalism. All the emotion in the world is not going to produce the fervent quality of "it is done." It will only produce a temporary stimulation which will eventually leave you cold and without hope.

Emotion is merely the quickening of the human consciousness to a point of passion. You may imagine you are very spiritual, but nothing happens. A flower blooms because it cannot do anything else, and so and so and so. When will you see the glorious ease with which Jesus moved? See how quickly after he had fed the multitudes he moved on. He did not stand in a daze and invite personal worship or personal following. He kept telling his hearers to "follow me," the Father within.

"When ye pray," you do not need to find out how it is done from a man—all is told. When you pray, go in and *shut the door*. You don't take any rules or organizations or men into the secret place; you shut the door, and when you have done this, the Father-Consciousness "which seeth in secret shall reward thee openly." In other words, it will work—just what you have been trying to do for so long.

Again, there is no mystery. Jesus spoke the word, raised the dead, opened the eyes of the blind with no human excitement on his part. He went on to the next thing without having to be glorified, yet was the power glorified in each instance. Wonderful, his abandon. No

Without the Smell of Fire

one to write him up and tell what a wonderful teacher or healer he was, because he kept telling them, "The works that I do, ye shall do also, and even greater." So will it be with you when the Christ has come for the second time and you have experienced it in the flesh and have exclaimed, "Yet in my flesh shall I see God." *Yet in this very temple-body shall you see God.* Do you want to see anything else? If you once see this, will you have need of seeing anything else? What think ye?

"Verily ye shall be fed." Don't worry, you will have what you can take from the kingdom, no more, no less, and what you can take is what you can recognize as "it is done." Your degree shall be according to your *recognition*. What you accept comes to abide with you; what you reject passes you by. What do you accept? Do not measure it by the findings of another or past attainments or failures. If your tent is not large enough, you alone will have to enlarge the borders, and if you are tired of scratching your feet on the sharp pebbles and shells of the shallow waters of personal teachings, you will have to "launch out into deep water."

It is wonderful, wonderful. Yea, "heaven and earth are full of thee." Do you understand? Do you grasp the materialized *word* of God? It is here and *now*, and it is *you*. You are the word of God made flesh; hence you are free into heaven. The Lord's Prayer was answered before it was said, but it will never be answered until it is a reality to you—an actuality, an *it is done* state of consciousness.

"Knock, and it shall be opened unto you." Do you believe this is possible because it is already open, and the confident knocking is the accepting of the kingdom of heaven on Earth? "Ask, and it shall be given unto you." Is that so? Can you ask and receive because you have already received? "Seek and ye shall find" because everything is

The Answered Prayer

right here. But all this is foolishness to the human mind, and that is exactly what it should be.

The wisdom of God is foolishness to the human mind and vice versa. The wisdom of man is nothing but an accumulation of human opinions and beliefs that will pass away. In a few years, man will laugh at what he believes today and will say he has outgrown his childish beliefs, yet will the *belief* in God remain eternally the same. There is no changing of this wonderful thing, but all that you believe in today from a human standpoint will be swept away later on. So why not be in advance of the parade and see through this nothingness.

"Well, I want to, but ..." And so the old personality practically says there is something stronger than God, in spite of all. What say you?

"Call upon me, and I will answer you." Is it so? Or is it? You answer and argue about it or "go in and possess the land." Walk free from it all and *let* this glorious manifestation come through into visibility. "Thy kingdom come" is the lament of the human mind until it becomes the pure recognition that Thy kingdom *is* come here and now, and from this flows the infinite substance of Life.

Be still, then, and *know* that *I* am God. Not manufactured by human thought, but *am* God here and now and will remain so forever, no matter however many planes of human reasoning you pass. *I* am he that should come—do you hear? Or look ye for another? You have to answer this. Your little greediness measured by the human wants must be given over to the infinite substance of All, where there is no need for greediness. It is wonderful, moving out of the limited into the unlimited Presence. Too long have you been separated from Me. Cast off this limitation and come out into the infinite Spirit and know and appropriate the Presence. It is wonderful

"Eye hath not seen, nor ear heard, neither have entered into the heart of man, the things that are prepared" for those who love the law. The loving of the law is your alignment with the principle of *it is done*. Then the old Adam cares and fears are gone forever. You understand that the limitations of Adam are of such narrowness that they cannot see or hear or appropriate the gifts that are prepared. You do not have to make them; they are prepared already. Do you want them, or do you want to make a demonstration of the Adam-consciousness to prove to another that you have more understanding than he has? Do you want spirituality in order to gain more prestige with a handful of human beings and to fill your coffers? Watch … be still … do, have, be, take, ask Me, receive, believe. Just a few little words for you to guard.

Your prayer has been answered.
It is well with thee. Do you hear?
Answered before you ask.

NOTES

You make your own road signs at night by letting your light so shine on them that they become visible. They are there all the while but are not visible until your light touches them. Do you understand how it is that all things are there, even the answer to your prayer before you ask, but it takes that "let your light (of recognition) so shine ..." Do you begin to see the difference in trying to make things happen, and just letting them come into place? Wonderful, isn't it?

* * * *

Once in Spain, I saw an old lady going down the road carrying an enormously large bundle. I stopped the car, and after some assurance that I was all right, got her into it, the first one she had ever ridden in. She was going to her little home some thirty miles away. It would take her two days or perhaps more. Can you imagine the state of her mind to find, thirty minutes later, that she was set down at her cottage? Breathless, filled with terror, and in confusion. She had experienced a miracle as far as she was concerned.

Something that ordinarily takes two days to perform with hard labor was accomplished in thirty minutes. Nothing to you? Why? Because you are quite familiar with speed of motors. Ever think you might step up your sluggish consciousness and find some things as natural that now seem to be miraculous? God is still *wonderful*—and so are you. "Awake thou that sleepest, and Christ will give thee light," just as you gave your road sign light at night. Are you thrilled? I am, when I think about it all.

Without the Smell of Fire

The next time the old lady in the story went to church and heard the priest tell about Jesus being over at the other side of the lake instantly, she could understand it. Can you? Step up a little. Come out from among them; I have something to say to thee. "This day shalt thou ..." Do you hear? Do you want to be in paradise with Me this day? In paradise, where you do not have to steal enough to live on. Do you? Wonderful, isn't it?

* * * *

A son of a rich merchant of India, on arriving at maturity, said to his father, "I would be a holy man." So the father gave him his substance and sent him forth.

Twelve years later (maybe it was eleven, or maybe it was thirteen, or maybe it was less—shall we stop here and argue about the history of the case?—we generally do), a lean, haggard-looking individual approached the home place. The father came forth and greeted his son. "Well, son, what have you learned in all your twelve years?" (Or eleven or perhaps ten, or ... shall we stop here and begin that again? You see what I am trying to put over to you? Perhaps a little foolish, but just the same ...)

And the young holy man said, "I have learned how to walk across the Ganges."

"What?" said the Father, in great surprise, "you have taken twelve precious years to walk across the Ganges when the ferry only costs two cents?"

Ever meet anyone who had spent forty years doing good things that could all have happened without the bother? Ever find one who had denied himself everything to become holy and had made himself so holy that no one could stand him?

Wonderful, isn't it? The mirth of God, the joy of breaking down that silly old idea that God is a long-faced old tyrant and spends His time sitting about trying to catch you in some evil. The glorious laughter of God, the joy of Life and Light, the lovely words "Beloved, now ..." "Feed my sheep" are all you need to *hear* the laughter of God ringing through the world, breaking the old forms and patterns of human thinking. Wonderful, isn't it?

FEAR

The thing I feared has come upon me.

By fearing it, I gave it the force and power to embody itself in something evil and hateful. The childhood fear that creates a boogeyman out of thin air is not quite as ridiculous as the adult fear which creates out of thinner air a figure or set of situations which will not only bring tears to his eyes but will also actually annihilate him.

If you were to tell a man who was fearful that he was giving to the thing feared all the power it had, he would no doubt laugh at you, for the "thing," be it person, place, or object, might be completely detached from him. In fact, he might even protest he had never even thought of it before. It is of little moment to him that thousands of people live in the same universe with him who are neither afraid nor mindful of the thing that petrifies him with fear.

The reaction of everything in the universe is a result of your attitude toward it. Everything must and does act in accordance with the power you give it. The level of consciousness at which you function draws for its support on the accepted race consciousness of the thing.

Hence, a savage, believing that electricity is the power of an evil god, would be backed up by the conscious thinking of everybody at that level, and this, together with his own fear, could precipitate the evil of his belief. Yet millions of people dwelling there in the same world would laugh at his fear and would denounce the results as self-hypnosis. The moment he "saw" the truth about electricity, he would drop all fear of it as a power of a strange god. He could then acquire the reverence (fear) of this newly discovered substance and respect its laws, knowing that as long as he cooperated with these laws he could count on harmonious performance of many wonderful things.

All fear of evil is engendered by the belief in two powers, one good and the other evil, or the distorted belief that God has the capacity to curse or destroy His own creation. The whole of creation is *God Himself*. Cursing, damning, and all the other horrible beliefs attributed to God are not in accordance with the law that God is Love. If God is the only power in the universe, then everything you see in the universe is God in action, befogged as it may be by a belief in evil. You have only to recognize this Presence to shatter the evil belief appearances. Even hell must give up when you realize that "if you make your bed in hell, there am I." If *I* am there in the midst of hell—then it is heaven.

All this simple teaching is for the consciousness that can "believe" and that has lost much of its double-sighted, double-tongued wisdom. If you can, you can—do you hear? If you can *find Me* in the midst of the evil you are sustaining by your thought, *I* will appear to you, and that is the end of the evil. The belief pictures which you are throwing on the screen of Me are cut off. Nothing has happened to Me. Here am *I* in the midst of you. It is wonderful. Praise the Lord.

You endow the thing you are afraid of with all the power it has over you. A doctor normally is not afraid of morphine or other poisons; he handles them with impunity. But a drug fiend is scared of them, especially if he is trying to break a habit of drugs. This shows definitely that habits cannot be successfully broken unless fear of the thing is removed. Then he, the victim, does not run away from the thing he has endowed with power. He discovers it powerless to affect him. Every cell of his mind is cleansed of the desire for the drug the moment he sees this.

Without the Smell of Fire

You cannot run or hide from the thing and thereby free yourself from it, for it is within you and will embody again. But once you have taken away the belief in its power, it has nothing more for you. A person whom you have endowed with evil over you is only operating because of your belief in evil. Every time you think of him, you give him more and more power over you, until finally he comes upon you. But once you take away this power through the recognition of Love, then will you perceive that he disappears from your life as an evil influence. But it makes no difference whether he goes or stays; you are free from it all.

Fear of poverty brings out a whole reel of pictures of the poverty, keeps you from getting a job, and holds you out of expression. This, of course, only takes place in the hypnotized thought realm. You as the spiritual being can never be out of your place. This is not an affirmation that can be made to happen. It is something that is so and will have to be *recognized*. Once the *fear* of poverty is deleted and you move out into the God-substance, the pictures that make up poverty will disintegrate before your eyes, and you will go to the level and degree of substance you are able to recognize.

It is amazing the power that can be given to an inanimate thing. Jewels have been, in some instances, the apparent cause of death, accidents, and evil of all sorts because they were believed to possess evil powers. In one instance, after a long series of evil events had taken place attributed to a certain jewel, it was found that the original jewel had been pawned and a cheap substitute put in its place, but with the same power. "Red brings me good luck," says one; yellow makes me sick; blue is healing." What do you think? If blue healed, all we would have to do is to paint all hospitals blue, and the doctors would be out of a job.

Fear

Do you see what all this is leading to? It is leading you to the magnificent power that is already yours. Not a power to use—you *are* that power. You will eventually see this and "decree."

"Well, I cannot help it, thirteen is unlucky, say what you will," and so it goes, and you have the support of everybody in the race who thinks as you do. But there are those who reverse this and say, "Thirteen and black cats are lucky" … and so ….

Do you begin to glimpse why Jesus, discovering the reservoir of power within himself, knew his freedom to such an extent that he would risk the sum total of race consciousness and go through its most final belief, "death"? So are you beginning to see the power of the Christ and how it is that now this permeation of the two, Spirit and body, is actually bringing forth the "God in the flesh" through which all things are to be manifested and brought into being. It is wonderful!

"The thing I feared has come upon me." It has not come upon another—it has come upon me because it has been in me all the while, and finally I have magnified it and contemplated it within myself to such an extent that it has taken on a body and form.

The giant of the Philistines is a picture of fear embodied. The David is the awakened consciousness with its five spiritual senses that bring him down. David destroys the mental (thought) structure of the giant, and he collapses. If you have already gone so far that you have put your fear on Earth and made a reality of it, you can destroy the thought structure of the giant and see the embodiment crumble to dust. The moment you shut off the stream of thought feeding him, he will begin to totter, and presently, as he has spent the last bit of energy given him, he will disappear. This can happen to the most adamant thing or belief in your life. It is wonderful how you now can take away all life from your fear giant, no matter what his name may be. You have come to the new day—the former things and order have passed away.

Do you begin to note that most of the schools of metaphysics are starting at last to take up the idea that thought will do nothing? In reality, they are only finding out what Jesus taught two thousand years ago. For years the central theme of the teaching has been "think, think, and think," and thereby do what Jesus said could not be done by thought. But now are we in the last days, and every stone shall be thrown down until not one stone shall remain upon another, and the headstone of the corner of Jesus Christ shall be set in place. All the old beliefs are wearing so thin and are so worn-out they are exposing their own impotency. The power of the drug has gone—it is nothing but personality and psychology.

Organizations so often start with the premise "God is Love" but end by introducing a heterogeneous collection of fears which cause the members to lose all sense of freedom. I have met many people, in what they called the Truth, afraid to leave their organization—which was supposed to heal, help, and love—because of the evil that would befall them. What of all this? Ask yourself. Awake from this separated sense of life. Enter into the oneness and be free.

A case in point happened daily in a San Francisco building. Two ladies who were in the business of Truth used to be controlled by a girl of another faith. It often happened that whenever these two ladies who professed one Power decided to go downstairs, the girl in question left her office at the same time. Then the two ladies were obliged to turn around and go back because the girl had another faith. The simple little girl was quite unconscious of the power with which she was endowed, but she operated it over two somewhat husky ladies. Why? She controlled them—but *they* controlled God! And so it goes. Who or what is keeping you from going down in the elevator of life when you want to? What? Is that so?

Remember, fearful one, that even Jesus was powerless to do good unless it could be accepted. Do you believe that some personality, condition, organization, no matter however important he or it may be, can cause evil to happen to you? Will you answer whether you believe evil more powerful than good? Do you know of anyone who had more power than Jesus? And yet in some places "he did not many mighty works there because of their unbelief." If good cannot be forced upon you by Jesus Christ, the great power of the universe, then will you not understand that evil cannot be forced upon you unless you *believe* in it? And your divine indifference to it causes it to return to the source of its own creation.

If the thing you feared has come upon you—stand up to it. Don't run from it. Take away the belief structure of it and see it fall to the ground, a heap of dust. Remember, pay tribute to no personality. No personality is worthy of anything more than your respect.

Remember, the moment you break the thought flow to the evil you see, at that moment you have shut off its life power. The thing you feared comes at you again only to run full onto the sword of Revelation and thereby destroy itself.

THE WAY OUT

Destroy this temple (body), and in three days I will raise it up ... I can pick it (the body) up and lay it down ... Your body is the temple of the living God.

The entire havoc that man has experienced has been through believing the body possessed intelligence and power apart from God. The body as we know it is the only thing in the universe capable of experiencing evil, for it has separated itself from the One and has wandered into a far country of belief, opinion, history, and fear.

All these pseudo powers have their origin in judging from appearances. Appearances are the results of seeing, hearing, touching, smelling, and tasting the universe through the distorted material senses. Not one of the unenlightened senses can give an accurate or true report of anything. The so-called mind of matter is "a liar and the father of it," having no power of its own but to create illusion.

This confused mind has a set of vicious laws wherein it sees good and evil, admitting that God is omnipotent, at the same time finding the devil more present and more powerful, "As for man (separate from God, or living in a body consciousness), his days are few and full of trouble." He shall earn his living "by the sweat of his brow." Small wonder, then, he finds himself feeding among the swine, the symbol of human beliefs.

"Now through a glass, darkly, but then face to face." As long as man conceives of separation, he will experience the distorted conditions of matter, and not until he discovers his permanent Identity, Father, will he be able to arise from this consciousness of frustration.

The Way Out

As matters stand, no material man "can pick it up or lay it down," for the reverse is the truth. The body can and does become sick, infirm, aged, and apparently can pick it (man) up and lay it down. And no matter what mental protest or affirmations he makes, the body can and does take a man out of circulation by causing him to be sick, poor, unhappy, all against his will, and man can do little or nothing about it.

True, some of the man laws are not exactly fatal, and if the man works hard and follows all sorts of human laws, he may get rid of the disease, but there is nothing sure about it. What cures one may kill another. "One man's meat is another man's poison." There is no assurance that anything the human mind knows will prove even half-way successful, although applied with integrity. He may shut his eyes to it all and imagine he is going through experiences that will "do him good," or that God wants him to suffer, or something of the sort. Sometimes he sinks to such a level as to imagine there is "purification through suffering," yet even while acknowledging this, he is trying with all possible force to get rid of the suffering. Yes, "there is no hope in him" as long as he maintains this separation and this dense ignorance of his permanent Identity, or Father within.

Presently, however, he begins to remember, and this memory of something that has been causes him to arise finally from the pigsty of human intelligence and go to his Father. His eyes are suddenly opened, and he begins to hear the words of Jesus: "I can of mine own self do nothing." He suddenly discovers the body to be an unintelligent mass of atoms controlled by consciousness and which at no time control consciousness. "As a man thinketh in his heart, so is he" becomes an open sesame to the king's treasury. He has discovered the difference in *heart* and *head* thinking.

Without the Smell of Fire

Man has been thinking so long with the head brain that he has forgotten the heart brain, which does not *try* to produce strange and wonderful results or manifestations, but which announces the fact that they are about to appear. The head brain then becomes the servant of the heart and is able by this cooperation to carry the mechanics through to results undreamed of and quite impossible before.

The following is an excerpt by Benjamin DeCasseres, *Los Angeles Examiner*, 1939:

> You thought your brain was in your head. That's right, but that is only one of your brains. You have another brain, according to the famous surgeon, Dr. George W. Crile.
>
> Recent advances, he says, have shown there is another center, a second brain, in the nerve center in the region of the heart. This center is even more powerful than the head brain because it controls the many miles of the circulatory system as well as respiration and digestion.
>
> And Dr. Crile might have added that it also controls our thoughts in the head brain, for as I pointed out in this column from time to time, the brain in the head is only a converter into consciousness of our wishes, our instincts, and our secret prejudices.
>
> Thus all our thoughts are wish-thoughts, and I salute Dr. Crile in having the courage to put the origin and center of our thought-life into the heart region, for the proverb that says "as he thinketh in his heart, so is he" is actually and scientifically true.

When the awakened man begins to "see" just what the body is, he begins to understand "destroy this temple, and in three days I will raise it up." He then can literally begin to "pick it up or lay it down," for he finds it to be more or less in the nature of a mirror into which is thrown the consciousness he has "remembered." The body merely reflects what is in the consciousness, and that is why the body cannot be changed by thought any more than the reflection in the mirror can be altered, for there is nothing that can be done to change this reflection until that which is causing it changes.

Now, the mirror reflects all the human thoughts, and man has set about trying to change the picture instead of the thought. This old human thought is the idea of separation that leads man out of the Garden into a place of "free will." His free will has landed him in a dungeon against which he protests, "You cannot put me here, because I am innocent." But the jailer answers, "I know, but we have you here." The hopelessness of it brings such frustration and futility that man runs and hides his head in the sands like the ostrich is supposed to do.

When man discovers his permanent Identity as "himself" and not something he uses, then the mirror (body) begins to take on an entirely different aspect. In place of disease, it suddenly manifests health; in place of poverty, it pictures wealth, and so on. In the twinkling of an eye, and as this contemplation of the Father takes place and man begins to see the attributes of God through his permanent Father-Consciousness, he is able to change the entire shape, outlook, and form of the reflection of the body (mirror). It is amazing how the recognition of anything in the Father causes the man (body) to change instantly and bring out the "picture shown to him on the mount." This process is past the reasoning of man, for it is the way of God, which is past finding out through thought. It is wonderful!

"Ye must decrease, I must increase." Eventually the power is entirely taken out of matter, and matter is then found to be an unintelligent mass of atoms ready to take on the consciousness and to perform the works of God. It is only when man sees and understands the helplessness of this body that this very same body can accomplish that which it is utterly incapable of performing. For now it is

Without the Smell of Fire

coming under an entirely new set of laws, some of which are almost impossible to put in words, and none of which can be understood by the human intellection. Who can understand the miracles of Jesus which took place because of the mind which was in him—and which is also in you? The command "Be still, and know that I am God" then takes on a rich and deep meaning.

The moment you discover your Father-Consciousness as *you*, you are able through this connecting link to contemplate God and the things of God, and the body (mirror) then begins to take on the new reflections of harmony, wealth, and health *to the degree* that you can accept them as natural and possible. It is wonderful, how this Light suddenly melts the hard-fast belief which has bound you for so long and wipes out the idea that you can make God do your bidding through praying at Him.

Hence, "though a man were dead, yet shall he be made alive" is true and just. The moment the body is seen to be merely the mirror of reflection, the end of much of the difficulty has taken place. The hard-fast nature of evil melts before "the brightness of his coming," and old laws and patterns which have been held true and eternal are wiped out with ease because they are found to be pictures cast into the mirror by human thought.

All this is not a thought-taking process. You cannot think yourself into anything but more evil, because "who by taking thought can add one cubit to his stature" is true. It is not willpower or affirming or studying lessons. It is pure recognition of the fact that you have a permanent Identity within you which is your real Self and which is your point of contact with the universal God. It was this permanent Identity called "Father" to which Jesus turned and asked, or called upon, in order to change the picture on the mirror before him. Hence, when we see him performing his so-called miracles, we find him instantly retiring

The Way Out

unto the Fatherhood degree of Consciousness and then suddenly bringing out the new reflection.

The old prophet who put his hand in his bosom and brought it out white with leprosy and, repeating the same act again, brought it out whole and well, knew that his body was a mirror upon which was cast the picture of consciousness. Man, who separated himself from God—even as you and I—began to accept these pictures as the reality and to build up laws and histories about them, and finally to become so hypnotized by them that even God seemed to be a great deal less than omnipotent. It is wonderful how we are discovering the facts of Life through the revelation of Jesus Christ.

Gradually the light will dawn upon you that the temple of man, the entire manifestation, is nothing but a series of mirrors onto which are cast the pictures of your degree of consciousness; hence, what you see in the world, you have conceived in mind. Therefore, a man may be a devil to you and a saint to another, and you may see disease, murder, theft, poverty multiplied by as many mirrors (bodies) as are in your universe. Whatever is in your consciousness is in your universe and is caught up by all the mirrors about you. No one can come to you with any belief whatsoever that is not in your consciousness, however much you may fight against this and however much you may want to destroy the idea. *If it were not in your consciousness, you could not see it or experience it.* It has to be in your consciousness for you to be able to recognize it. That is the only place it exists, and that is the only place from which it can be eradicated.

Hence, when Jesus saw hunger in himself, he saw it in five thousand others too. Every mirror (body) gave forth a picture of hunger and backed it up by supposedly intelligent proof. Then he retired into the consciousness of his Fatherhood degree and found there no such a thing as

Without the Smell of Fire

lack or hunger, and now the picture of his consciousness suddenly cast another reflection on all the mirrors, and they were fed.

So is it with everything in your life. It cannot be changed from without. There is nothing you can do with matter; you can change nothing from the matter standpoint. Working with the body and the affairs on the outside is a poor proposition. Understanding your permanent Identity and assuming the power which is yours through our Lord Jesus Christ, you can change the picture, and hence the reflection will also change. You break the pattern of the human thinking, and the reflection changes immediately.

Nothing can or will stay in place in your life except it be held there in consciousness. As soon as it is dropped from consciousness, it is out of the only place it ever existed, and the reflection will disappear just as it does in the mirror when the object before it steps out of proximity of the mirror. It is as simple as that. Believest thou this?

Thousands of people have tried to demonstrate health, happiness, and prosperity and have taken endless courses of lessons to show them how and yet have found themselves caught in the web of failure. Jesus showed in hundreds of ways that all this working with the outside of the "platter" whilst the inside was full of uncleanness was no way to get results.

Do you begin to see why "I and my Father are one" causes the changes to take place in the (mirror) body which otherwise could not have happened? There is no reason to it, and the more you try to reason it out the further you go from the simple revelation of the Master. It requires *recognition* of your *union* with God through the permanent Identity (Father) within. The moment you sense this, you will be able to change all discord in your life and bring out the impossible.

Remembering this, you stop railing against the pictures shown to you in the (mirror) bodies of the world. They are merely catching your state of consciousness, good, bad, or indifferent, and once this is glimpsed, you will stop fighting against the immaterial thing called matter and understand perhaps for the first time why you are told to "put up your sword." If you fight any longer, it is because you are still separated from God and are in a "far country" of beliefs, battling against reflections which cannot possibly change, because of something in your consciousness that holds them into place.

When Jacob discovered this, he "loosed it (the picture to which he had been holding all night) and let it go." In other words, he discovered that the very thing he was fighting with was created and sustained by his own thought. If you continue to fight with the sword, you will perish by the sword, for you are fighting an illusion which you are endowing with greater and greater power all the while.

Now anything is possible to you, and you can easily understand why you can "go" now and do the works of your Father, because the whole universe is a mirror which is to reflect the consciousness of God you have accepted as true and real.

Knowing this, "Go then into all the world" and take no thought about the scrip, the purse, the robe; do not bother with the body, what ye shall eat, or the raiment, for now you see that all these things are quite naturally reflected into position by this new elevation of "I and my Father are one" and the recognition that the universal Father-God is greater than the individualized Father *you*.

You are returning to the Eden you left, lo these many years, and finding the kingdom of heaven here and now.

It is wonderful.

REVELATION

To use an illustration: *consciousness* is likened to the water in a basin; *manifestation* the cork floating at the level of the water. The raising or lowering of the water level automatically affects the level of the cork. It is something over which the cork has no control. If the water is calm, the cork remains likewise. If the water is agitated, so is the cork, and nothing it can do of itself will change the condition. The cork has no control over the water, its movement, rise or fall.

Take the body of man as the cork, the consciousness of man as the water, and you begin to understand that at no time can man in any way control consciousness, but may express its every whim, register its every mode. No amount of work, either physical or mental, is going to change the relative position of the cork. If it were possible to endow the cork with sight, we should readily understand that the outlook and the elevation of this outlook would depend entirely upon the level of the water.

Making a demonstration might be likened to changing the level of the cork by throwing it into the air and imagining that it has momentarily gone to a new level by its own effort. Almost before it has time to take cognizance of the new state of things, it has returned to the former level with a great splash and a great need of readjustment.

"With all thy getting, get understanding." The first and foremost step in all this is to recognize, once and for always, the utter impossibility of body (man) doing anything of himself. Cast out of your mind the pseudo-truth that man is a creator, a sub-creator, or a helper of the divine Power. Man (man-ifestation) is of himself entirely without power. Jesus represents man: "I can of mine own

Revelation

self do nothing." The cork cannot rise or fall without the water level being changed.

The seemingly independent action of man is his erroneous belief that thought can and does do something. All the wisdom derived from thinking is foolishness in the eyes of God. Nothing except belief is changed by thought. All the thought in the world cannot act upon a thing and change it or its nature. Hence, all the knowing and thinking in the world at one time did not make it flat. Yet as far as the majority of people were concerned, at that time it was accepted as flat. However, one glimmer of light, and the entire working basis of their lives was swept away. In reality nothing was changed. "Who by taking thought can add one cubit to his stature?" If not this, then why try other and more difficult things? Awake thou that sleepest, and Christ (Consciousness) shall give thee light.

Nothing can exist to man until he recognizes it. He can recognize only realities; all else is illusion created out of thought substance.

When all the world (your world) knows poverty, it is as real to you as the flat world was to the world in Columbus' time. But that doesn't make it so, for the infinite substance of the Presence exists in all its abundance; yes, all the while you are figuring from the thought elevation, poverty is a very real thing to you and to thousands of other people. At that level, the cork sees exactly what it accepts. This acceptation is backed up with ample proof that poverty is a reality. Once the consciousness is changed, once the level of water is raised, the outlook of the cork, or man, is also changed. "Whereas before (on that level), I was blind—now (at this new level of consciousness) I can see." It isn't so strange, then, that Jesus counseled "Be still, and know that I am God," that the nature of this Consciousness be entered into instead of the vacuity of human thinking.

Gradually man stops trying to demonstrate or use or make this Power do anything and glimpses the alignment that is to take place. Of course, he cannot approach this in human thinking and reasoning, for it is a lie to human reason. The moment you try to reason God as a reality, you find you have nothing but formula. When you dissect a body to locate life, you find only death. To think that God can prosper you is to think a lie, for it is not so. Nothing can possibly happen by thinking. When you see something beautiful, you do not have to *think* it is beautiful in order to make it so. You become conscious of beauty, and then thoughts flow freely from the new recognition that it is beautiful. Thought does not create anything—in its rightful function thought flows from consciousness.

A sick man is usually in a sick world. He knows thousands of other people who are sick and wonders where they came from. He is at that level of consciousness where it is the truth to him, and he sees it everywhere, reads about it, hears of thousands of cases that verify his suffering. At whatever level you stand, human thinking will partake of all the race consciousness of that degree. Likewise in the spiritual degree of unfoldment, you partake of all of the blessings that are already yours.

The fable of the greedy dog perceiving the reflection of the bone he holds in his mouth, thinking it to be larger than the real bone, does exactly what the human thinking does—drops realities and grabs at shadows.

Looking at the *symbol* as reality instead of the consciousness back of it results in the same thing, and man gets the sharp rebuke: "You seek me after the loaves and fishes and cannot find me." You always find a man without loaves and fishes, and so when you seek God with the idea of getting something out of Him, He suddenly has nothing

Revelation

and becomes a nebulous substance called Spirit, which is perfectly helpless to assist you in any way.

The belief that you are studying truth in order to learn how to demonstrate things, even health, is a mistake. This wholesale mistake is being shown to the world now. After years of instructions in how to get things, no results are forthcoming. Yet that very power invites you to "go in and possess the land" and tells you, "Now ask, that your joy might be full."

All this study of God in order that you may make a financial demonstration is a base deception and will not result in anything but disappointment. Yet in reality, you should seek Him for nothing else but manifestation. Through the beautiful blending of Jesus and Christ, we perceive that Jesus (man) is the place of expression for Christ (Consciousness) and that over it all is the universal Cosmos, God.

Seeing that this wonderful revelation is given to the child and that only the child can enter into the kingdom of heaven takes away all the straining and trying or worrying about the mechanics of it. It is a glorious relaxation when you glimpse even faintly the revelation of consciousness. It will take away all the excitement of trying to make things happen and will "judge not from appearances" anymore, but turn the attention to the consciousness and the magnifying of it.

Mary knew this secret perhaps better than any other recorded character, when she "pondered these things in her heart." She did not think of them in her head. For the moment, she tried to think about this impossible thing taking place and was lost in a sea of adverse testimony and hateful situations over which she had no control. But staying on the contemplation (in her heart) of the Presence gave her the consciousness of it all, and the mechanics took care of themselves—the child was born.

So will it happen to you when you stop trying to make demonstrations or trying to do things on the outside and turn your attention to the one and only teaching, that of Jesus Christ. Release every person, book, organization, etc., out of your life. The more you can find a thing true in God the more possible it becomes with you.

From the thought basis of man, how can he answer such a question as "Believest thou that I am able to do this unto you?" He has already thought and known it to be entirely impossible, yet here is a question to be answered. In every instance where it was answered in the affirmative, it was productive of results instantly.

At first we may contact this consciousness a little intermittently, as the old human thought rises so easily, but as we "ponder these things in our hearts" we shall begin to see also the "before they ask, I will answer," for we shall see-feel from the point of consciousness that it is so and that it is done.

Without this faith "it is impossible to please him." The pleasing is merely the alignment with the power which causes it to work out smoothly and naturally. Without the knowledge of the laws of mathematics, it is impossible to work out a problem, even though the answer already exists. Do you begin to see the reason for "be still, and know that I am God," and how you have entered now into the new lesson which is so simple and wonderful and yet so difficult because we want to "think" it out?

God's promises are kept, and they are free to all. They offer infinitely more than the best promises of man, yet because man tries to make these promises true, he fails to function them. "To him that hath shall be given" is not unfair; it is an automatic functioning of consciousness. No person who is still seeking to make isolated demonstrations can expect to gain anything but an intangible sense of the coming and going of good. No sooner does he demonstrate a thing than it begins to go from him and he has to go back again, and usually the second sign is not forthcoming.

Why do you seek to demonstrate God by bits? Why not the whole garment? Why not begin the conscious recognition of the Presence in everything and everybody—here, there, and everywhere? You cannot do this through the human thinking, for it is impossible and will only cause confusion and chaos.

"I go before you to prepare the way." The water rises, and the cork rises with it. God goes before to prepare the way, and man functions at that point of recognition. It is wonderful!

HOW IT IS DONE

And he said unto him, because thou hast been faithful in a very little, have thou authority over ten cities.

The moment man recognizes the Presence, he automatically begins what seems to the human sense increase. In reality, the recognition of the Presence is all that is necessary to bring out anything desired. If you can find it possible to God and impossible to yourself, you have set the rudder in perfect position to carry you into the port of fulfillment.

Most people, after having set the rudder and not seeing the port the next instant, give up. The rudder sags, and ere long they are miles out of the true course.

In the parable of the various servants being left a sum of money to invest and increase, we see the varying degrees of reward coming back to them, and all start with the one point of recognition. So you may increase your recognition until you are made ruler over "ten cities"—ten states of consciousness, all different and all heavenly—or you may be made ruler over the fulfillment of your own negative words.

To the one who had merely kept the talent entrusted to his care, came the cursing of futility. Standing in the way of recognition and saying such things as, "Yes, I see, but why doesn't it work?" ends in just this reward. The very questioning in the case answers itself. How can a man possibly see increase? Do you see a plant grow literally? No, you notice that it has happened after the growth has taken place, yet all the while you are conscious of its actual growing. Unseen in front of your very eyes this action takes place, for you, "having eyes, see not."

How It Is Done

If you cannot *accept* it, it cannot come to pass, for only that which you can accept can possibly be fulfilled. But even this acceptance will not give it a body, for the thing must grow into the full stature. So we find that the recognition is the first step. Before it could possibly happen in any sense of the word, it would have to be recognized as *being*. The acceptance then brings it a step closer, for now you are at the place where you believe it could happen to you, and no matter what the appearances are, you still accept the fact that it could happen to you. You do not know how, and if you try to find out, you kill the seed. "No man knows, not even the son but the father," so no man, with the most highly developed sense, can tell how the Power is going to work out the situation. Ask no man.

So we find first the recognition of the Presence by Mary. She was overshadowed with the Presence, felt It, recognized It—and then we find her natural doubt about the proposition, even as you and I might doubt the fulfillment of a thing which seemed quite as impossible. Yet eventually we see Mary accepting the idea. She was in a quandary as to how such a thing could take place, but instead of trying to find out, she pondered these things in her "heart-brain." She did not think about them; she *pondered* them—mulled them over, became one with them, seemed to touch-sense them as realities—and after this, finding it still impossible as far as she was concerned, she knew there was only one thing to be done: glorify and magnify the power. So Mary, after pondering these things, knew that if it were to take place it would have to be done by a power entirely above the frail limitations of her human self.

By acquainting herself with this Power, she knew in her heart that "I have a way ye know not of," that the Father-Consciousness within her had accepted this as possible and was now in contact with the universal God, and this perfect hook-up could and would bring it to pass in a manner and by a means that no man knew or could know.

"Acquaint now thyself (you—I am speaking to you, the reader) with him, and be at peace: thereby good shall come unto thee." What have you to say about this becoming acquainted with the Power? Answer me—you who are constantly seeking things. Here is the way of obtaining all of them. Acquaint now thyself with Him and be at peace: thereby *all* good shall come unto thee. Do you want more than all? Well, how much more? And do you still try to make this thing work by your human thought, which is even now saying it is impossible? The voice of God speaks a magnificent truth. The thing you are trying to do is quite impossible. Your personality has done everything it possibly could to make it happen. Yet in the face of all this, you can bring it to pass. The impossible thing becomes a reality.

Do you see the need of recognizing the Presence instead of trying to do something about it? God cannot be operated as a stage character. He is not a man but a principle, and unless the hook-up is correct, there is no chance for Him to come into visibility. This sounds very much as if God were under the control of man, but He isn't, any more than the laws of mathematics are under the control of man. Man can only experience them as he becomes one with them. Then he is mathematics in operation, and the more he magnifies this law the more he can enter into the unanswered, abstruse conditions of life and bring out perfectly astounding results.

No one thinks it odd that a man magnifying the law of mathematics can work through unsolvable problems. Without recognition and the acceptance of the law, man could never do the impossible. From the human standpoint, the more he magnifies or contemplates the power

How It Is Done

of mathematics the more abstract it becomes, until it is sheer relativity.

If this is true of mathematics, so is it true of music and art and everything else. It is much more true of the world of Spirit. The moment you begin to make the assumption of this truth, it actually becomes a part of you and is not *used* anymore. This power of recognition brings to light the unseen—embodies it. No matter how long the law of mathematics has existed or how perfect it may be, without man to express it, it is nothing. Man actually becomes one with this law and thereby is the law, just as Jesus said, "I and my Father are one." Yet he also knew that "the Father is greater than I." The more man magnifies the law of mathematics the more the things called problems become merely equations of life wholly solvable.

Human thought which has failed to accomplish anything puts on a cloak of false modesty and says, "Who am I to do such a thing?" The answer is "Yes, who are you?"

The power of God is far removed from all the trivia of human illustrations. God-power is so much quicker than human motion, so much more entirely outside of any thought or human contemplation.

If you cannot *recognize* the presence of God here, there, and everywhere, you cannot often meet the situation into which the human thought has thrown you. You cannot see how you can gain the substance needed unless it be by the sweat of your brow. The saying of words or affirmations, the holding of thoughts or clinging to the personality of another is now proven worthless.

"Come unto me, all ye that labor and are heavy laden, and I will give thee rest." Do you hear this invitation, you who are worn out trying to demonstrate health, happiness, or money? Do you hear, and do you understand what this Me is, that to which you are to go? It is found in the heart-brain, in the place of recognition, that *feel* which can *accept* it as possible even though everything in your outward world testifies to the falsity of it all.

Do you begin to *sense* now that strange thing that happens when you can answer in the affirmative the question, "Believest thou that I am able to do this unto thee?" Do you *sense-feel* something now that was formerly vague and impossible?

Can you recognize with the sense-feel consciousness that if it is possible to God, it has already taken place? Can you come to the place where you accept it as possible to you, even while your human thought is knowing it is utterly impossible? If so, can you magnify the power and ponder these things in your heart, keep silent and let them grow through the slow or rapid processes of the human thinking?

Do you hear? Do you understand why the servant was given ten cities over which to rule? And how the curse fell upon that one who just kept the idea in his mind and did not push his recognition to the place of acceptance, then magnify the power to such an extent that he could proclaim finally in face of all the adverse testimony, "I have gotten a man from the Lord," and then be able to "show John" his manifestation?

"Who did hinder you, that you should not obey the truth?" What—a system, an organization, a teacher, lecturer? Who did hinder you? When will you answer, "I hindered myself because although I recognized this wonderful Presence, yet I could not sense-feel that it was possible for me, and hence I was cursed with the barrenness of my own words"? Nothing is truer than "ye shall eat your own words." It is a poor diet when these words have been as negative as most human minds concoct.

Can you begin to acquaint now thyself with *Him* and be at peace? Why don't you try it? You have acquainted yourself with the human thought-taking processes and

How It Is Done

been in the hell of human fury all these years. Now then, nothing worse can happen by acquainting yourself with Him and being at peace, and suddenly—ah, miracle of miracles, you are experiencing the revelation: thereby all good shall come unto you. All good—every bit of it—shall come unto you here and now.

It is so wonderful and so glorious that now you are walking out on the waters of your old fears and are magnifying the Power to such an extent that you are "entering in." The secret shell of silence shall hide thee during thy labors until the child is delivered in glory and light and you proclaim from the housetops of your consciousness, "I have gotten a man-ifestation of the Lord."

From glory to glory—it is wonderful.

BEWARE OF PICKPOCKETS

My house shall be called of all nations the house of prayer; but ye have made it a den of thieves.

Today in the Temple at Jerusalem, one sees religions bought and sold, as any other commodity, in the open market. Religion is a business, prayers are formula, and lucky charms and amulets are hawked with much avidity. A candle is thrust into your hand and lit for you on entering, and money is demanded fiercely for this "gift" as you leave. The mumbling of dozens of creeds and rituals and the odor of incense fill the atmosphere—the Temple erected to the eternal memory of Jesus Christ. And lo, the signs: "Beware of pickpockets."

It is not a far cry back to the time of Jesus, when he entered the Temple and overturned the tables of the money-changers and drove forth those who sold doves and oxen. "Why make ye my Father's house a den of thieves?" That it is recognized as a den of thieves is evidenced by the fact that the warnings are posted to protect one against them.

"Why don't they do something about it?" asked one devotee, who stood aghast at the farce that was going on in the name of Jesus Christ.

We keep on asking this question, until we suddenly reveal to ourselves why nothing is done about it.

"Destroy this temple, and in three days I will raise it up."

"Impossible—it cannot be done. It took years to build it, and you say it can be restored to its perfection in three days." But!—and the revelation that follows opens the door to why something is not done about it. He spoke of the temple of his body, and the moment we get this clearly in our consciousness, we will see that the cleansing of the Temple of the thieves does not refer alone to the material temple.

The driving of the moneychangers, the merchants, and thieves from the material temple was only an object-lesson for those who had to learn that way. It was merely a dramatization of what must take place in every man. This, however, cannot take place until we realize that the temple is the embodiment of your ideas, which you call a body. When you begin to realize this, you begin the cleansing process, and the moneychangers and thieves are scourged out of your consciousness.

The beliefs in evil that are doing business in your temple—the thief of time, writing his "one day nearer the tomb" constantly, with a relentless energy; the thief of procrastination, collecting unborn happiness while you wait eternally for the day of joy to arrive; the thief of anxiety, stealing away "the peace that passeth all understanding," which is a gift to you—all these thieves, and many others, are suddenly driven from the temple, and it becomes the "temple of the living God," filled with Light and Life.

This is the temple of the living God. Your body is that temple, and that Light and Life are permeating the body, searching the joints and marrow; penetrating the dark crannies and recesses of the mind and lighting them up with the radiance of the noonday. Down come the smoking lamps of rite and creed and the odoriferous incense pots, for the Light has come, and in the coming of this Light there is no place for the thieves to hide, and so the signs of warning, "Beware of pickpockets," also come down. There is nothing within the temple to attract them, and there is nothing that they can, or could, take. In the light of this inner Lord, they are found to be shadows of outgrown beliefs.

Formerly, "confidence men," who followed in the wake of a traveling circus, used to announce from the platform that their show was endeavoring to give the people the highest form of entertainment, and also to protect them from all trickery. For this reason, the "bawler" asked everybody to beware of pickpockets. At this warning, every spectator casually made sure that his valuables were safe.

This was exactly what the accomplices of the bawler wanted to know; it saved them time to see the exact location of a man's valuables, and the rest was comparatively easy. In the very desire to protect himself from the thief, he drew the thief to him, and so it is with all the beliefs from which we suffer.

Remember that if there are no signs in your temple, "Beware of pickpockets," it will not be because there is nothing of value in the temple; it will be because you have come to the understanding of the Presence, which does not permit this action of dishonesty to take place in your consciousness. There is that hidden in this Power which withers the faintest desire to steal, and so the pickpockets, or thieves, finding no warning against them as a possible means of entry, pass by. The pickpockets of health, prosperity, joy, and all of these thieves, finding no recognition, fail to enter into the temple. It is wonderful how the Light has come through.

"But if all these pickpockets, thieves, moneychangers, and evildoers are within ourselves, how is it that Jesus could have experienced them?"

"Nothing happens but my love allows" is the answer to this question.

Jesus made it quite clear that he had power to release himself from the Crucifixion if he so chose. "Thinkest thou that I cannot now pray to my Father, and he shall presently give me more than twelve legions of angels?

Nothing happens but My love allows. So in order to bring out the nothingness of evil in its worst form, he submitted to death. Yes, it is wonderful—because he showed us that even the "last enemy" could, and should, be overcome; that the temple could, and should, be cleansed of the thieves, and the signs "beware of pickpockets" should be made null and void—of no use as far as we were concerned—for in this temple of the living God, there was no place for thieves and no possibility of their getting in. The pure Light proceeding from the throne of God, passing through the flesh, resurrects it from the death of beliefs and makes it a tower of shining, luminous Light.

"Thinkest thou that I cannot now pray to my Father?" Remember how the Master always called attention to the fact that "the Father within, he doeth the works," to reassure you that you have the Power within yourself—within your own consciousness, within your temple—and when this is roused or awakened, the thieves of joy, health, prosperity, and those that traffic in prayer, or the word of God, go scurrying out into the darkness of oblivion.

It is wonderful! Wonderful! Wonderful! "Ye are the temple of the living God." "Behold, the tabernacle of God is with men." "The Lord thy God in the midst of thee (not another) is mighty."

It is wonderful when you begin to recognize that you are the temple of the living God and that out of the temple proceeds the glorious light of freedom and understanding, and from the altar of your being flows the stream of Life, crystal pure and sparkling, which when a man drinks thereof, he shall never thirst again. And from the hidden recesses comes the hidden manna, dropping down from heaven, of which a man may eat and live forever.

Come without price and eat and drink. The invitation is to you, the starving one, who has been so long out in the material belief world, undernourished with the few grains of wheat you could glean from the husks of life. "Come and eat of my body, and drink of my blood" is the invitation which many pass by because it seems almost absurd, and at best only a religious wording of an idea. But you begin to understand what it is to partake of this holy meal—the substance of Spirit and the inspiration of God. "The flesh and blood of Spirit" seems a strange way of putting it, but it is the glorious "substance of things hoped for," and it is the "inspiration of the Almighty" coursing through you into expression, bringing you freedom from the years of bondage and the terrible scourge of the hard taskmaster which says, "by the sweat of your brow."

If you are still feeding on the bread of material learning and belief, you will have to earn it by the sweat of your brow, under the terrible lash of the human taskmaster, belief in evil. But the invitation stands eternally, and one day you will stop eating the bread you earn by the sweat of your brow and begin to partake of the living Bread that cometh down from heaven—and remember that heaven is a state of consciousness, according to Jesus.

The reason we have so long fed upon the bread we earned by the sweat of our brow, the bread which "your fathers did eat in the wilderness (of beliefs of evil) and are dead," is because our temples have been full of thieves, and our best efforts to protect ourselves from the pickpockets proved worthless. The temple must be cleansed—your temple, not the temple of some other person whom you believe needs it more than you.

Don't be misled by the old fable any longer. Look within and start now the cleaning process. This doublemindedness, believing in good and evil, must go. And how does it go? By fighting evil or hoping to overcome it? No, it disappears in the light of Truth, just as shadows are absorbed by light. The contemplation of the Light within

Beware of Pickpockets

causes It to become more and more real to you, and this "be still, and know that I am God" is the very means by which the Light is released into expression. It is wonderful!

Your body is the temple of the living God, and it is filled with Light. Naturally this Light proceeds out from it, and quite naturally healing and help take place without the conscious effort to make these things take place. Just as evil has seemed to function in your life when you would have done good, now, with the coming of this light into the temple, does good begin its automatic functioning into expression. It is wonderful!

We begin to see this automatic functioning of the Power which operated through Jesus, and how it was that he kept calling our attention to the fact that It is impersonal and impartial, instantly available to anyone at any place. We begin to understand why it was that the woman who touched the hem of his garment received her Light, or healing, and how it was that "virtue proceeded out of him." The perfect agreement which another makes with the Light in you causes this action of Spirit to take place, and the world says a healing is made, but in reality something that has been eternally in existence has been revealed. The Christ is not a teacher—he is a revelator of that finished kingdom of heaven.

The kingdom of heaven is at hand.
Believest thou this?

Ask yourself this question. Do you believe it? Do you think it has to be re-created by any man, any teacher, any system of ideas invented or brought out in these later times? Answer it for yourself. Can you stand up to the question *Believest thou this*?

In the quiet of your soul, ask yourself this question. It is the searchlight which, when turned onto your temple, will expose a whole band of thieves hiding back of the

Without the Smell of Fire

sign that you have erected: "Beware of pickpockets." Do you believe the word of God? Or would you just like to? Enter into your temple, and with the scourge made of the best Light you have gathered, put forth these thieves that are taking from you the priceless heritage. *Believest thou this?*

Do you believe anything you have read thus far? That question must be answered by yourself and for yourself. It is wonderful, this candor and honesty of the consciousness that is fearless to stand up to the words and ideas it is saying. "Be not afraid, it is I." The noise and confusion of the host of thieves, pickpockets, and merchants leaving the temple is nothing to be alarmed about. "Arise, shine, for thy light is come, and the glory of the Lord is risen upon thee."

It is wonderful to contemplate this golden Consciousness which is even now awaiting your acceptance. You can say within the secret place of your being, "I believe in God" and mean it, feel it, see it, and experience it in your body, in your universe, in the whole of Life. It is wonderful the way this glorious Light is streaming from you in all directions, causing the shadows of material beliefs to flee away into nothingness.

It is wonderful for you to be still and know that *I* am God in the midst of thee. It is wonderful for you to be still and watch the coming of this glorious Soul into being; the Solomon entering his temple not made with hands and releasing the Sun into expression, around which moves all the universe; the great flood of Light emanating to every part of your temple-body, transmuting it into the resurrected substance of which Jesus spoke and which he demonstrated.

You, the reader, sitting quietly by, shall experience the glorious baptism of this Light, this awakened Soul, and your temple shall be cleansed of the thieves, and your

Beware of Pickpockets

body shall be like a well-watered garden, saturated by the Life-giving waters and the substance and power of God.

There is nothing to worry about when you begin to recognize this Presence and when your consciousness has come to the impersonal-personal willingness of "Send me, Lord." When you recognize this Solomon in his temple and are willing to do the Father's business, then you have nothing to worry about, for "it is your Father's good pleasure to give you the kingdom of heaven," and great is the joy of the awakened soul. It is wonderful!

Such a radiant peace and calm come over you. A quietness possesses your soul—an active inactivity, a resting in action, a radiant, vibrating, pulsating Life omnipotent. "In quietness and in confidence shall be your strength." "You shall not need to fight; set yourselves ... and see the salvation of the Lord."

It is wonderful! Wonderful! Wonderful! "Bless the Lord, O my soul (senses), and forget not all his benefits."

It is thrilling to contemplate the transformation that is already taking place on the unseen side of your life because you have renewed your mind. The parasites of belief that have been living on the substance of your thought are destroyed, and all this lovely Power is turned into new channels of expression. "Bless the Lord, O my Soul, and forget not all his benefits." How can you forget them when you are flooding over with the joy that comes from the Light which is pouring through every nook and cranny of your being?

It is wonderful! Wonderful! Wonderful! Blessings! Blessings! Blessings all about you, here, there, and everywhere. You are a radiant song of joy and gladness because *I* came "that your joy might be full."

"I will stand upon my watch," to see what He will say unto me. Not what He will say to another, but what

Without the Smell of Fire

He will say to *me*. He has something to say to you. It is wonderful to contemplate.

Ye are the temple of the living God, filled with Light and Truth. Virtue is proceeding out of you to all mankind, and in the light of this virtue the kingdom of heaven is revealed.

Take down your signs, "Beware of pickpockets." There is nothing to fear in all God's kingdom; there is so much of the substance, when realized, that there is no need for anyone to steal. The automatic action of this newly recognized reliance shows.

THE INSPIRED PRESENCE

"The inspiration of the Almighty, when it has come unto you, shall lead you into all things." It leads you straight into the inspired Presence in which the old idea of start-stop, begin-end ceases to exist, it being a limitation of the manifest world.

The inspired Presence is eternally in expression. It comprehends no beginning or ending, as does the manifestation. Things come and go, but the inspired Presence in which you live and move and have your being, when you are awakened to the Divinity within, lives and moves and has Its being in you.

In the mental, unenlightened world, we live on a plane of demonstration where a little health is made manifest, subsequently to lapse into sickness; a little wealth followed by limitation. But in the inspired Presence, to which Jesus was constantly calling attention, there is no coming or going. The Spirit is constantly in action and in manifestation on the unseen side, and it becomes a never-ending stream of manifestation when man aligns himself with It and gives It a chance to express.

Hence, when the statement is made that "man is always in his right place," this is true and eternally so, provided he is aligned with the Power. There is, then, no getting out of expression or loss of expression. It may change, as the infinite, impromptu pattern of Spirit brings to him a newer and higher flight of manifestation, but from that instant he can never be in and out of the expression of Soul. It is wonderful to

The Eyes of the Blink

contemplate the presence of Spirit—the presence of this inspired Substance called God, and the escaping from the mental plane of coming and going.

Formerly man thought that by prayer he caused God to come into action or that he started the Power into action. When once he is awakened to the inspired Presence, he knows that the start and stop processes of life are gone forever, for there is no place he can go where the inspired Presence is not expressing to Its fullest. That is why Jesus said, "Take no thought" for the journey, the purse, the robe, knowing that the taking thought was the anxiety and fear that they would not, or could not, be made manifest at some distant point. Awakened to this Presence which is inspired and which leads him into all things, man knows that the moment he aligns himself with the God-Life through the recognition of the Presence, the invisible manifestation becomes visible, and the inaudible becomes audible. It is impossible to start and stop God. And God is all Life is.

The old idea of demonstrating a job or a place in which to earn a living gives way and entirely falls into disrepute in face of this marvelous revelation of Jesus the Christ. The jumping from one uncertain demonstration to another, like Eliza in *Uncle Tom's Cabin* jumping from one block of ice to another in an attempt to reach safety and freedom, is entirely a mental idea of God and does not even approach the constant, ever manifesting power of the inspired Presence. The contemplation of this Presence will cause you to see the utter impossibility of being out of place or out of expression.

Once his mind is relieved of the burden of *trying*

The Inspired Presence

to make something happen or *trying* to get into expression, man will relax in the divine activity of finding his expression going on always. He enters in and comes out at pleasure, but the Power goes on forever. He may withdraw or retire, so to speak, but the Divinity is constantly in expression. The command "Cast your burden on the Lord" takes on a new and delightful meaning. The terrific effort of holding himself in place subsides, and the inspiration of the Almighty leads him into new and lovely patterns of Spirit.

Once you are aligned with the Power, you cannot stay the endless manifestation and outflowing of the substance. The flowing of the substance through Jesus was no more difficult for five thousand than it would have been for one. As long as the consciousness is aligned with the Presence, the inspiration keeps leading the body into all things.

It is wonderful to contemplate the ways of God. "His ways are past finding out." No man can designate the precise manner in which the manifestation shall take place or through which temple it shall come forth. The great secret, "I have a way ye know not of," is the sure and certain way out of any and all difficulties, for it is the way into the inspired Presence in which there is no starting or stopping of the Power. A constant stream of manifestation goes on always.

You are moving in this inspired Presence—in the midst of this *Thee* of which it is said, "Heaven and earth are full of thee"—full of the substance of God, full of the inspired Presence, willing and ready to come into expression at the slightest invitation. "Behold, I stand at the door and knock" is but a line of poetry until you understand it is the urge of Spirit pressing

The Eyes of the Blink

upon you for expression, the inspired Presence seeking a body—seeking embodiment through you.

At the place of meeting with the inspired Presence, all things are suddenly reversed. Man no more thinks of God as healthy or wealthy, these being terms with which the mental limits Life. Life—God—is not rich as man thinks of riches. He is not healthy or well. These limitations will be dropped off with the mental "working" plane of thinking.

In this inspired Presence in which you live, move, breathe, and have your being, all of the qualities you tried to make true by demonstration are part and parcel of the grand whole. The effortlessness of life—the glorious, radiant, untrammeled *expression*—takes place without pomp or ceremony.

In this place of the inspired Presence, the only office of man is to accept and let the manifestation take place through him. He finds the inspired memory in the inspired Presence, and in this memory is the entire substance of consciousness ready and waiting to be called into action by recognition. The simplicity of this stupendous idea must be as automatic and natural as the coming of dawn. The moment any thought is taken on the subject, it becomes vague and hypothetical and impossible, and it seems to recede into nothingness. If you cannot accept the gift and use it freely, then no amount of begging or beseeching will bring it to pass.

The glorious impromptu pattern of the Presence causes old beliefs in human destiny, with their evil pictures, to break up and pass away and allows the divine destiny to come into instant manifestation. If you be in the Spirit—the inspired Presence—you are

The Inspired Presence

no more under the "curse of the law." Note the word *curse*. The law of belief, with its hard and fast destiny and its evil path of problems, is the curse that continually operates upon the man who is "working" with the Power instead of coming into *alignment* with the Power and *letting* It have the same glorious freedom of expression that we see in the record of creation. "And God said, Let ...." Whatever He said had to be *let* into expression. Whatsoever this very Lord speaking within you says must also be *let* to come forth in its own way and after its own unexpected design.

The Lord speaks to your Lord constantly through the means of desire and says, "I will give you the desires of your heart," but man will not, because he has a "start-stop" idea of God. Sometimes he thinks God is in expression and most of the time not. All this veil of human thinking and dual powers must be eliminated in order that the one Presence, the inspired Presence, may give you the desires of your heart.

Do you believe it is possible for you to have the desires of your heart? Perhaps they have become so distorted and twisted that you do not recognize your desires in their primal purity and beauty and have found none of them possible. When you align yourself with the inspired Presence through the recognition of the *One* here, there, and everywhere, then you will know that the desires fall into manifestation as the pictures fall upon the motion picture screen.

There is no conscious effort in the inspired Presence; the desires are given you as fast as you are able to take them. It takes a big, free spirit of Life to begin to take good. We have so long been schooled in evil and the traditions of misfortune or the necessity of problems for spiritual growth that we are surprised at the simplicity of the inspired Presence and continually return to the old cast-off ideas and try to make it work for us.

When you begin to feel the Presence here, there, and everywhere, you will understand what a glorious thing it is to be in the Spirit. "Cast your burdens on the Lord" and go free. Do you hear? *You*, reading this line, are invited to come into the consciousness of the inspired Presence, and from that moment you will move in a path of inspiration. "This is the way, walk thou in it." Turn to the right, turn to the left. Everything you do, everything you say, everywhere you go will the inspiration guide you. "I will walk in you and talk in you" becomes a fact and is no longer demonstrable in the old way.

You have cast the whole burden of thinking your way out of the human intellect on the Lord, and you are going free into expression. You are moving with the inspired Presence and moving into the impromptu patterns of your divine destiny. In this Presence you are free from the curse of the law, no matter how intense or how evil it has been.

This inspiration of the Almighty coming into you is the life stream passing from the invisible into the visible. It is "stepped down," as it were, into visibility. The door has been *opened*, and He who knocked for admittance is entering into an eternal expression. Do you begin to understand the living, moving, and having your being *in the One* instead of outside It? The duality of life gives way before this inspiration, and the possibility of the fulfillment of God's promises is seen.

"Without faith it is impossible to please him" sounds like a personal teaching. It is only put in the simplest form to bring it down to the most darkened understanding. It is impossible to please God (allow His power to be released) without the absolute acceptance of this Presence here, there, and everywhere—in hell, in your worst enemy, in the most iniquitous pit conceivable. We are beginning to see what Omnipresence, Omnipotence and Omniscience mean.

Is God everywhere actually, or is that just a theory you have been following? If He is everywhere, does that mean *everywhere* to you, or does it still mean that God is more present in certain places that man has especially sanctified?

If God had not been present in the mass of corruption in the tomb of Lazarus, no Lazarus could have come forth. If God had not been present in the tomb of Jesus, crucified as his body was, then no resurrection would have taken place. If God is not found in hell, devil, sickness, death, then these things will persist in their own individual way, living and sustaining themselves by your thought. It is wonderful when we begin to approach this *Oneness* and drop the dual nature of God and man.

No wonder Jesus appeared so void of sympathy. Knowing that the inspired Presence was everywhere, in everything—the lowest sinner and the highest priest—why should he feel sorry or condone the evil of belief, knowing that the recognition of the Presence would instantly shatter the beliefs of evil manifesting as a separate power?

You are beginning to move into the inspired Presence even *now*—yes, farther into it than you think.

The Eyes of the Blink

The invitations "prove me and see" and "enlarge the borders of your tent" are but encouraging words indicating that you can and will eventually recognize this inspired Presence and cause the manifestation to come forth in a greater and more glorious form.

All the old seeking for the how and the why and the methods of healing fall by the board. Never will the Power express twice in the same fashion—Spirit's infinite variety will take care of that. No two manifestations of God are identical; no set word or affirmation will heal all cases of a given sort. Hence, you see that in coming into alignment with the inspired Presence you discover you have automatically done the right thing, said the right word, given or withheld for no apparent reason whatsoever.

You are beginning to see why you were told to "go thou and do likewise" and how the false modesty or fear of the human mind began a series of questions and objections. "The former things are passed way; behold, all things become new," and so the old questioning gives way.

You will not be called upon to do anything you cannot do perfectly if you align yourself with this inspired Presence, and the performance of it will be after the manner of inspiration, which will make it definitely original and keep it entirely out of the path of competition, compromise, or opposition. Your expression will be the one and only expression of its kind—not that it may not resemble many others, but it will have that peculiar "something" about it which causes the world to say "success," which is merely the automatic expression of the inspired Presence. Do you begin to see what is the height, breadth, width, and

The Inspired Presence

majesty of this Presence of which Jesus spoke so often? "God works in a mysterious way His wonders to perform." Then why waste any more time trying to find the "how" of the expression? "At a moment you think not, I come." At the moment you align yourself with this Presence and drop off the thinking of the how and why, does this inspired expression come into manifestation. Endlessly and without beginning is the power going on. You may have been out of step with it and hence find yourself in a far country, or you may be sitting at home in the midst of all manifestation, but until you make the gesture, you cannot feel the action of this Power.

The brother of the Prodigal was downcast because of the fatted calf and complained to the Father. "Son, all that I have is thine; thou art ever with me." There is no report made that he "heard" this, because if he had, he would have risen up and given a banquet himself. You are told, "All that I have is thine," but that doesn't do anything until you realize that when a thing is offered you, you must *take* it.

Most of us go about complaining of our prodigality or our abundance, never using either one of them. When you *arise*, you do not have to go anywhere physically, but you certainly do go somewhere in Spirit—straight into the alignment of the inspired Presence—and the Father, seeing you a long way off, comes towards you. The manifestation instantly begins to come into the picture, and it flows steadily until every empty measure is filled.

I like to contemplate this being in the inspired and inspiring Presence—that everything you do or say is blessed automatically and that everyone you contact is blessed automatically whether he accepts it or not. You shall go in and come out and "find pasture." It is wonderful to know that your going in and your coming out (states of consciousness) carry eternal, automatic blessings, transmuting everything.

When you are doing everything automatically in the name or nature of Jesus Christ, you bring into manifestation the inspired Presence, and the Word then becomes flesh and dwells among you.

"I will recall to you whatsoever I have said unto you." *I* will recall the forgotten promises and words which you have lost in the plethora of human doings. Do you believe it is all possible, you who read this line? Can you *sense* this moving in the inspired Presence where the Power automatically works?

"My father worketh hitherto, and I work." The Power is always in motion, and when man recognizes this, he stops his puny efforts to make things happen and *lets* the glorious, inspired Presence express Itself through him; then he works, or carries out the mechanics, disregarding the limitations of the physical law imposed upon him by thought, birth, breeding, education, race, creed, nationality, or any other thing.

"Behold what manner of love the Father hath bestowed upon us." Have you beheld this glorious thing called Love which already has been bestowed upon us? Have you felt the Presence, and are you sensing this inspiration of the Almighty which is leading you into all things?

It is wonderful, dwelling in this inspired Presence with the inspired memory and the never-ending stream of life pouring out more than we ask or think.

"For in Him we live and move and have our being,"

and inversely, "For in us He lives, moves, and has His being."

> Oneness, Wholeness, inspired Presence—
> here, there, and everywhere.

ABOUT THE AUTHOR

Walter Clemow Lanyon was born in the United States in 1887 to British parents. He was educated in the United States, France, and England and spent more than half of his life traveling all over the world, investigating and studying the various presentations of Truth.

He is the author of some thirty-three books on Truth, a novel, two librettos for light opera, and innumerable articles and write-ups on human interest.

The simple manner in which Mr. Lanyon states the truth enables the reader to grasp the principle for himself and put it into practice without the sense of a personal teacher or organizational bondage.

He traveled and lectured to capacity crowds all over the world, basing his lectures, as he said, "solely on the revelation of Jesus Christ."

At one point, he underwent a profound spiritual awakening, in which he felt "plain dumb with the wonder of the revelation." This enlightening experience "was enough to change everything in my life and open the doors of the heaven that Jesus spoke of as here and now."

"*I know what it was. I lost my personality; it fell off of me like an old rag. It just wasn't the same anymore.*"

His prolific writings continue to be sought out for their timeless message, put forth in a simple, direct manner, and they have much to offer serious spiritual seekers.

Through years of proving the Word, he refined his presentation by eliminating the personal almost completely and leaving the pure revelation as simple and natural as possible. Thousands will testify to the tremendous spiritual force felt through the mere reading of his works.